Prepare for Grade 4

Second Edition

Summertime Learning

Prepare Your Child for Fourth Grade

Directions in Spanish and English

Editorial Project Manager
Eric Migliaccio

Editor in Chief
Brent L. Fox, M. Ed.

Creative Director
Sarah M. Fournier

Cover Artist
Diem Pascarella

Illustrators
Mark Mason
Renée Mc Elwee

Art Coordinator
Renée Mc Elwee

Imaging
Amanda R. Harter

Publisher
Mary D. Smith, M.S. Ed.

Teacher Created Resources
12621 Western Avenue
Garden Grove, CA 92841
www.teachercreated.com

ISBN: 978-1-4206-8097-3

Reprinted, 2024 (PO605322)

Made in U.S.A.

Teacher Created Resources

Table of Contents

Table of Contents *(cont.)*

An Important Message

El siguiente es un mensaje importante de la Asociación Nacional de Aprendizaje de Verano.

Estimados padres,

¿Sabían que todos los jóvenes experimentan una pérdida de aprendizaje cuando no participan en actividades educativas durante el verano? Esto significa que parte de lo aprendido durante el año escolar suele evaporarse durante los meses de verano. Sin embargo, la pérdida de aprendizaje se puede prevenir con la ayuda de los padres. El verano es la época ideal para participar en actividades interesantes y divertidas que ayuden a los niños a conservar y desarrollar sus habilidades académicas. Algunas ideas:

- Lean con sus hijos a diario. Visiten juntos la biblioteca local y escojan libros que aborden temas de su interés.
- Pidan a los docentes recomendaciones para la lectura de verano. The Summer Reading List (páginas 92–94 de esta guía) constituye un buen punto de partida.
- Exploren parques, reservas naturales, museos y centros culturales.
- Consideren cada día como un sinfín de posibilidades de aprendizaje. Medir las cantidades en una receta o estudiar un mapa antes de un viaje en auto constituyen algunos modos de adquirir o reforzar una habilidad. Utilicen las Learning Experiences que se encuentran al final de este libro para obtener más ideas.
- Establezcan metas a alcanzar de forma diaria. Por ejemplo, realizar cinco problemas de Matemáticas o leer un capítulo de un libro.
- Alienten a su hijo a completar las actividades de los libros tales como *Summertime Learning*, con el fin de reducir la brecha de aprendizaje que suele producirse en el verano.

Nuestra visión es que cada niño se sienta seguro, saludable y comprometido con el aprendizaje durante el verano. Para obtener más información, diríjanse a *www.summerlearning.org*.

¡Que pasen un verano *memorable*!

Matthew Boulay
NSLA Founder

Using This Book

Como padre, posiblemente sepas que el verano es una época para divertirse. Pero también puede ser un tiempo para aprender y prepararse para el próximo año escolar. Al combinar la diversión con el aprendizaje, los libros incluidos en la serie *Summertime Learning* pueden ayudar a tu hijo a mantenerse en el camino educativo y, a su vez, disfrutar del descanso físico y mental que tanto necesita. Con el fin de ayudarte a ayudarlo, hemos desarrollado un recurso organizado, flexible, práctico y gratificante.

Organizado

Summertime Learning: Prepare Your Child for Fourth Grade se encuentra organizado en torno a un período vacacional de ocho semanas. Incluye dos actividades para cada día de la semana. De lunes a jueves, dichas actividades consisten en una lección de Matemáticas y una lección de lectura o escritura. Los viernes ofrecen un divertido cambio de ritmo e incluyen actividades que se centran en habilidades tales como la creatividad, el pensamiento crítico, la capacidad de seguir instrucciones y la resolución de problemas.

Flexible

Hay muchos modos de utilizar este libro de forma efectiva:

- **Día a día**—Tu hijo puede realizar las actividades en orden, comenzando el primer lunes de las vacaciones. Para cada día de la semana, realizará las dos actividades designadas. (Consulta el calendario de la página 7).
- **A elección**—Si no quieres que tu hijo realice las actividades estrictamente en el orden en que están presentadas en el libro, puedes elegir una combinación de páginas acorde con sus necesidades e intereses.
- **De todo tipo**—Si sientes que tu hijo necesita más apoyo en un área que en otra, puedes optar por centrarte en las actividades de Matemáticas o Artes del Lenguaje.

Además, las páginas de este libro se encuentran perforadas, lo que permite arrancarlas en caso de ser necesario. Si se escoge este método, se puede decorar una carpeta y designarla especialmente para almacenar las páginas sueltas.

Extra Extra

- Para acceder a un práctico calendario que ayude a establecer expectativas y mantenerse al día, consulta la página 7 de este libro.

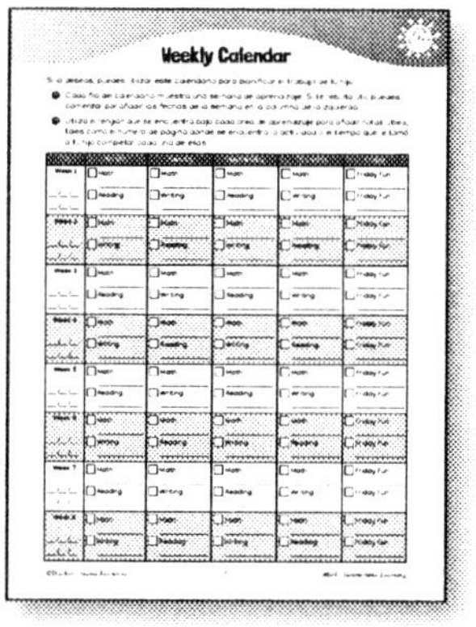
Weekly Calendar

- Para incluir más escritura en el programa semanal, consulta los "Journal Topics" en la página 8.
- Para conocer distintos modos de incrementar la lectura de verano y las experiencias de aprendizaje, consulta las páginas 92–97.
- Para páginas de referencia útiles en las áreas de letra cursiva, multiplicación y división, corrección, y mucho más, ver páginas 98–104.

Using This Book *(cont.)*

Práctico

Los padres desean páginas de actividades que no generen dudas sobre cómo utilizarlas, qué se espera que su hijo haga, y cuáles son las respuestas correctas. Las páginas de *Summertime Learning: Prepare Your Child for Fourth Grade* tienen como objetivo responder a esta necesidad.

En la parte superior de cada página de actividades se ofrecen distintos datos de forma directa y de fácil lectura.

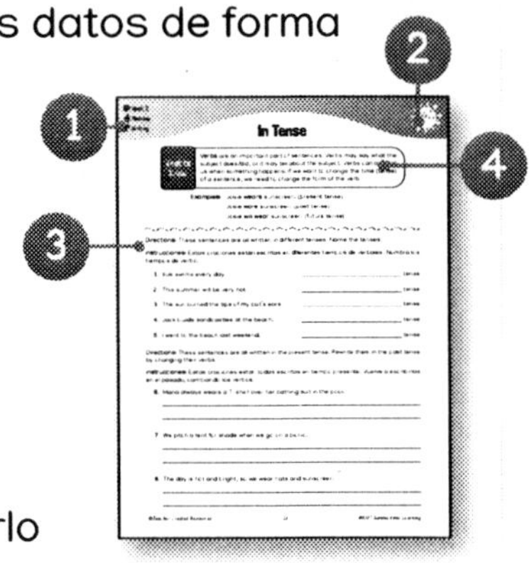

1. En un costado de la página de actividades, se encuentran el día de la semana y el área de aprendizaje. Esto permite a los padres verificar rápidamente en qué se encuentra trabajando su hijo y mantenerse organizados a lo largo del verano.

2. En el costado opuesto de la página figura un ícono de un sol. Constituye el sitio ideal para colocar una calcomanía y, de esta forma, hacer un seguimiento del progreso de tu hijo y recompensarlo cuando completa las actividades incluidas en el libro. Esta función también ayudará a orientarlo hacia las actividades del día siguiente. Al final del libro, encontrarán más de 300 calcomanías coloridas que podrán ser utilizadas para este fin.

3. Las instrucciones para cada una de las actividades se encuentran escritas de forma clara y de un modo que permita comprenderlas fácilmente. Muchas veces sucede que los niños poseen la capacidad de desempeñar una habilidad educativa, pero responden de modo incorrecto porque las instrucciones no son lo suficientemente claras o no han sido leídas en su totalidad.

4. Algunas páginas incluyen un casillero llamado "What to Know" que ofrece un recordatorio de la regla gramatical u ortográfica que tu hijo deberá saber para poder completar la página.

Además, al final del libro se incluye una guía completa de respuestas (páginas 105–111) que puede ser consultada cada vez que se tengan dudas sobre alguna respuesta.

Recompensas

Puedes utilizar el Reward Chart que se encuentra en la página 112 de este libro para realizar un seguimiento de aquellas actividades que ya han sido completadas. Esta página está diseñada para ser utilizada con las calcomanías proporcionadas al final de este libro. Cada vez que tu hijo finalice una página, puede escoger una calcomanía y utilizarla para rellenar uno de los círculos del gráfico.

Las calcomanías también pueden ser utilizadas en las páginas individuales. El sol que se encuentra en la parte superior de la página constituye el sitio ideal para colocar la calcomanía escogida. De este modo, será más fácil orientarlo hacia las actividades del día siguiente: pueden simplemente localizar la última calcomanía colocada y trabajar en las dos páginas consecutivas.

Hay suficientes calcomanías para rellenar el Reward Chart y añadir en cada página de actividades.

Weekly Calendar

Si lo deseas, puedes utilizar este calendario para planificar el trabajo de tu hijo.

- Cada fila del calendario muestra una semana de aprendizaje. Si te resulta útil, puedes comenzar por añadir las fechas de la semana en la columna de la izquierda.
- Utiliza el renglón que se encuentra bajo cada área de aprendizaje para añadir notas útiles, tales como el número de página donde se encuentra la actividad o el tiempo que le tomó a tu hijo completar cada una de ellas.

Day	Monday	Tuesday	Wednesday	Thursday	Friday
Week 1 __/__/__ - __/__/__	☐ Math ________ ☐ Reading ________	☐ Math ________ ☐ Writing ________	☐ Math ________ ☐ Reading ________	☐ Math ________ ☐ Writing ________	☐ Friday Fun ________ ☐ Friday Fun ________
Week 2 __/__/__ - __/__/__	☐ Math ________ ☐ Writing ________	☐ Math ________ ☐ Reading ________	☐ Math ________ ☐ Writing ________	☐ Math ________ ☐ Reading ________	☐ Friday Fun ________ ☐ Friday Fun ________
Week 3 __/__/__ - __/__/__	☐ Math ________ ☐ Reading ________	☐ Math ________ ☐ Writing ________	☐ Math ________ ☐ Reading ________	☐ Math ________ ☐ Writing ________	☐ Friday Fun ________ ☐ Friday Fun ________
Week 4 __/__/__ - __/__/__	☐ Math ________ ☐ Writing ________	☐ Math ________ ☐ Reading ________	☐ Math ________ ☐ Writing ________	☐ Math ________ ☐ Reading ________	☐ Friday Fun ________ ☐ Friday Fun ________
Week 5 __/__/__ - __/__/__	☐ Math ________ ☐ Reading ________	☐ Math ________ ☐ Writing ________	☐ Math ________ ☐ Reading ________	☐ Math ________ ☐ Writing ________	☐ Friday Fun ________ ☐ Friday Fun ________
Week 6 __/__/__ - __/__/__	☐ Math ________ ☐ Writing ________	☐ Math ________ ☐ Reading ________	☐ Math ________ ☐ Writing ________	☐ Math ________ ☐ Reading ________	☐ Friday Fun ________ ☐ Friday Fun ________
Week 7 __/__/__ - __/__/__	☐ Math ________ ☐ Reading ________	☐ Math ________ ☐ Writing ________	☐ Math ________ ☐ Reading ________	☐ Math ________ ☐ Writing ________	☐ Friday Fun ________ ☐ Friday Fun ________
Week 8 __/__/__ - __/__/__	☐ Math ________ ☐ Writing ________	☐ Math ________ ☐ Reading ________	☐ Math ________ ☐ Writing ________	☐ Math ________ ☐ Reading ________	☐ Friday Fun ________ ☐ Friday Fun ________

Journal Topics

Haga que su hijo elija uno de estos temas del diario dos veces por semana. En un diario o cuaderno, pídales que escriban algunas oraciones en respuesta al tema elegido. Recuérdeles que agreguen suficientes detalles para que otra persona que lea sus respuestas sepa lo siguiente sobre su tema:

Quién   Qué   Cuando   Dónde   Por qué   Cómo

Si lo deseas, puedes utilizar lo siguiente como herramienta de organización. Marca la fecha en que tu hijo completó cada consigna.

#1 a new holiday I'd create for people to celebrate Completed: ______________	#2 what a school designed by me would look like Completed: ______________	#3 what it's like spending the night in a new place Completed: ______________
#4 one of my talents Completed: ______________	#5 the best scene in my favorite book Completed: ______________	#6 one of my favorite trips Completed: ______________
#7 what a really good teacher always does Completed: ______________	#8 what I should probably be given an award for Completed: ______________	#9 the perfect day I'd plan for my friend and myself Completed: ______________
#10 what I like to do on weekends Completed: ______________	#11 a new invention I'd create to help fourth graders Completed: ______________	#12 what can be done to solve the problem of graffiti Completed: ______________
#13 the music I listen to when I want to relax Completed: ______________	#14 what my last argument was about Completed: ______________	#15 chores children should do to earn an allowance Completed: ______________
#16 one habit I would really like to break Completed: ______________	#17 one of my funniest experiences Completed: ______________	#18 the best and worst healthy foods Completed: ______________

Standards and Skills

Estándares Educativos

Cada una de las actividades incluidas en *Summertime Learning: Prepare Your Child for Fourth Grade* cumple con uno o más de los estándares educativos nacionales. Para conocer cómo se relacionan específicamente las actividades con los estándares básicos estatales, visita *http://www.teachercreated.com/standards.*

- Desplázate hacia abajo en la lista alfabética para encontrar la *Summertime Learning (2nd Edition)* series.
- Haz clic en **Standards** el link para acceder a TCR8844 Summertime Learning Grade 4 Standards.

Habilidades Introducidas y Reforzadas

Las actividades de *Summertime Learning: Prepare Your Child for Fourth Grade* tienen como objetivo reforzar las habilidades aprendidas en el tercer grado, así como introducir otras nuevas que luego serán desarrolladas en el cuarto grado. Dichas habilidades se encuentran enumeradas a continuación, y en las páginas 10–11.

Escritura

- Utiliza estrategias de escritura para distintos propósitos y contextos
- Utiliza estrategias para redactar, revisar y editar trabajos escritos
- Escribe un texto explicativo
- Escribe un texto narrativo
- Escribe un texto autobiográfico
- Escribe una respuesta a textos de no ficción
- Escribe una respuesta a textos de ficción
- Utiliza un lenguaje descriptivo para mejorar las ideas
- Escribe oraciones completas cuando se indica
- Utiliza la forma de párrafo por escrito cuando se indica
- Utiliza una variedad de estructuras de oraciones en el trabajo escrito
- Utiliza varias partes del discurso, incluidos sustantivos, verbos, adjetivos, adverbios, y conjunciones – en el trabajo escrito
- Usa correctamente la ortografía, el uso de mayúsculas y puntuación en composiciones escritas
- Evalúa tu escritura y la de los demás

Habilidades Introducidas y Reforzadas *(cont.)*

Lectura

- Realiza una vista previa del texto
- Establece un propósito para la lectura
- Hace predicciones simples sobre lo que se encontrará en un texto y confirma/revisa dichas predicciones cuando sea necesario
- Utiliza claves fonéticas y estructurales para decodificar palabras desconocidas
- Usa claves sintácticas y contextuales para decodificar palabras desconocidas
- Entiende el vocabulario de lectura apropiado para el nivel
- Comprende patrones estructurales u organización en textos informativos
- Hace modificaciones a las estrategias de lectura según sea necesario
- Ajusta la velocidad de lectura para adaptarse al propósito y al nivel de dificultad del material
- Entiende el concepto de trama
- Entiende el propósito o el punto de vista del autor
- Conoce las características que definen una variedad de formas y géneros literarios
- Tiene una comprensión preliminar del concepto de causa y efecto
- Hace conexiones entre los eventos de los cuentos y las experiencias personales

Matemática

- Utiliza muchas estrategias para comprender los problemas
- Entiende que la manera de representar un problema puede ayudar en la solución del problema
- Conoce el lenguaje de operaciones básicas
- Utiliza prueba y error para resolver problemas
- Conoce la diferencia entre información relevante e irrelevante al resolver un problema
- Comprende los conceptos básicos de la teoría de los números
- Entiende formas equivalentes de porcentaje, fracciones y decimales
- Entiende el lenguaje de las operaciones básicas

Habilidades Introducidas y Reforzadas *(cont.)*

Matemática *(cont.)*

- Entiende el significado básico del valor posicional
- Entiende la relación básica entre números enteros, fracciones, decimales y números mezclados
- Usa modelos para identificar, ordenar y comparar números
- Multiplica y divide números enteros correctamente
- Suma, resta y multiplica decimales correctamente
- Suma y resta fracciones simples correctamente
- Usa estrategias para estimar cálculos
- Realiza cálculos mentales básicos
- Determina el efecto de la suma, resta, multiplicación y división en el tamaño y orden de los números
- Resuelve problemas del mundo real que utilizan operaciones numéricas
- Selecciona y utiliza las herramientas apropiadas para las tareas de medición
- Utiliza estrategias específicas para estimar cantidades y medidas
- Conoce el lenguaje básico para describir y nombrar formas geométricas
- Entiende las propiedades básicas de las figuras
- Entiende que las formas pueden ser congruentes o similares
- Comprende las características de las líneas y los ángulos
- Resuelve oraciones abiertas simples que usan operaciones con números enteros
- Entiende que las ideas y los conceptos matemáticos se pueden representar gráficamente
- Sabe que una variable es una letra o símbolo que se usa para representar uno o más números
- Utiliza gráficos de barras simples, gráficos circulares y gráficos de líneas para organizar datos y hacer comparaciones

Carnival Math

Directions: Solve each word problem. Show your work.

Instrucciones: Resuelve cada problema verbal. Muestra tu trabajo.

1. The carnival sold 1,542 adult passes; 4,791 senior passes; and 9,148 children's passes. How many passes were sold? _______________ passes	2. There were 2,067 people waiting in line for the Ferris wheel. An hour later, 1,841 people were still waiting in line. How many people had their turn on the Ferris wheel? _______________ people
3. The popcorn vendor sold 5,076 tubs of popcorn. 2,291 of the tubs of popcorn did not have any butter. How many tubs of popcorn did have butter? _______________ tubs of popcorn	4. At the snack bars, 5,027 servings of cotton candy; 2,386 bags of peanuts; and 1,081 snow cones were sold. How many snacks were sold in all? _______________ snacks
5. The Hot Dog Hut sold 7,356 hot dogs. 5,861 of the hot dogs were on sticks. How many hot dogs were not on sticks? _______________ hot dogs	6. At the prize booths, the people were given 4,104 stuffed bears; 8,677 stuffed bunnies; and 3,437 stuffed pigs. How many prizes were given away in all? _______________ prizes

Rules of the Road

Directions: Find the meaning of each underlined word below. Using the Definitions Box below, put the letter of the answer on the blank line.

Instrucciones: Encuentra el significado de cada palabra subrayada. Usando el siguiente "Definitions Box", pon la letra de la respuesta en la línea en blanco.

Definitions Box

- **a.** absolutely necessary
- **b.** environment, area around you
- **c.** command, control
- **d.** tired, sleepy
- **e.** follow, do as others do

1. ______
2. ______
3. ______
4. ______
5. ______

"Listen up, drivers. Many of you are here because you have been caught breaking the rules of the road. That cannot be allowed. If you want to drive a car, it is very important that you [1]conform to certain rules and laws. You can't go too fast. You have to come to a complete stop at stop signs. It is [2]essential that you are aware of your [3]surroundings at all times. In order to [4]helm a motor vehicle, you have to be awake and alert. You cannot be [5]drowsy. You cannot be focused on other things. A car can be very dangerous if its driver is not paying attention."

Directions: Write the best underlined word from above that expresses each idea.

Instrucciones: Escribe la mejor palabra subrayada de arriba que exprese cada idea.

6. I'm in charge of flying this plane. ______________
7. I'm ready for bed. ______________
8. I'm going to do what everyone else is doing. ______________
9. I must study if I want to get an "A" on the test. ______________
10. I live in a big city that has tall buildings. ______________

Twists and Turns

Directions: An object can be rotated (turned) clockwise by degrees. To what degree was each item turned? Circle the answer.

Instrucciones: Un objeto se puede rotar (girar) en el sentido de las agujas del reloj en grados. ¿En qué grado ha girado cada artículo? Marca la respuesta con un círculo.

Examples:

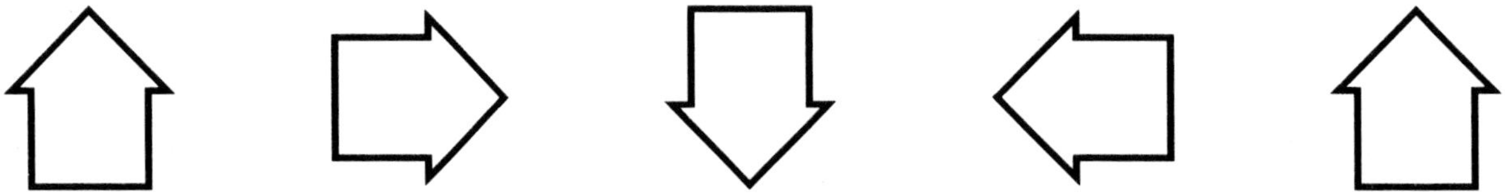

Start	90°	180°	270°	360°
	$\frac{1}{4}$ turn	$\frac{1}{2}$ turn	$\frac{3}{4}$ turn	full turn

1.

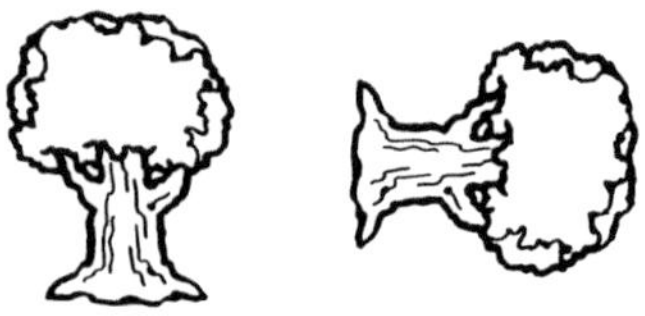

90° 180° 270° 360°

2.

90° 180° 270° 360°

3.

90° 180° 270° 360°

4.

90° 180° 270° 360°

5.

90° 180° 270° 360°

6.

90° 180° 270° 360°

7.

90° 180° 270° 360°

8.

90° 180° 270° 360°

9.

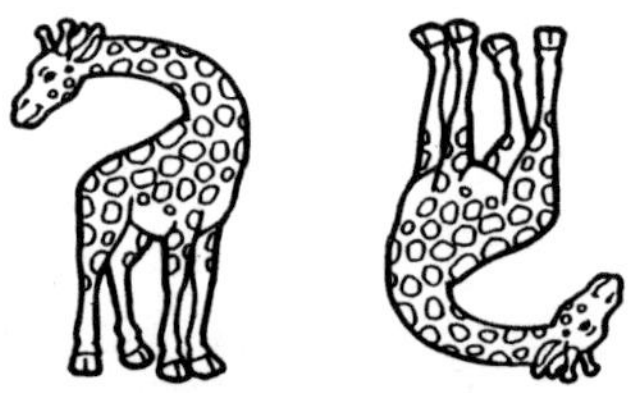

90° 180° 270° 360°

Cause and Effect

Directions: Complete the chart below. The left side of the chart is for the cause, and the right side of the chart is for the effect. Make sure that your answers make sense.

Instrucciones: Completa el siguiente cuadro. El lado izquierdo del gráfico es para la causa, y el lado derecho de la tabla es para el efecto. Asegúrate que tus respuestas tengan sentido.

Cause	Effect
1. I tripped on the steps at school. 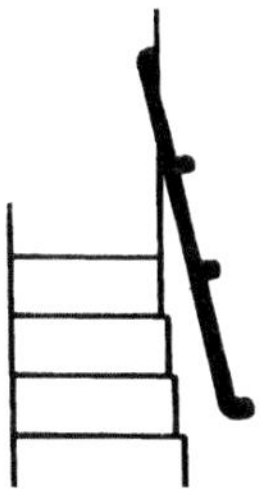	1. ______ ______ ______
2. ______ ______ ______	2. The dog was soaking wet! 
3. I scored the winning goal in our soccer game. 	3. ______ ______ ______
4. ______ ______ ______	4. My mom is very happy today. 
5. I completed my homework. 	5. ______ ______ ______

Make a Bar Graph

Directions: Using the information below, make a bar graph. Draw the bars to show how many hours a week these five children spend playing outside or watching television.

Instrucciones: Usando la siguiente información, haz un gráfico de barras. Dibuja las barras para mostrar cuántas horas a la semana pasan estos cinco niños jugando al aire libre o viendo la televisión.

Name	Outside (Hours)	Television (Hours)
Barbara	8	12
Joe	6	20
Jennifer	14	10
Michael	20	6
Sandra	16	10

Use the colors in the key below to make your bar graph. The first one has been done for you.

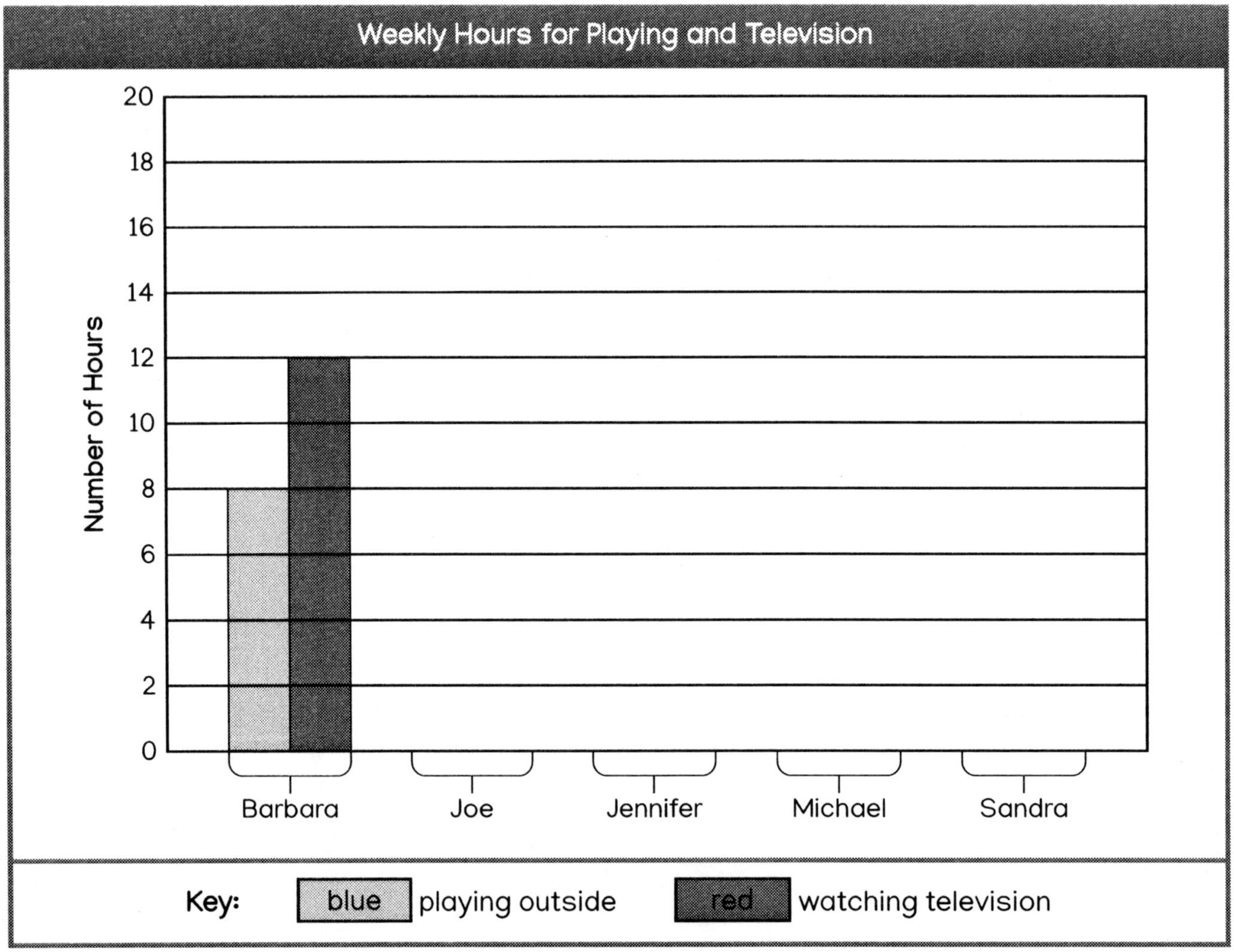

Tiger the Cat

Directions: Read the following paragraph. Then, identify the main idea and write two supporting details. Write them in the graphic organizer below.

Instrucciones: Lee el siguiente párrafo. Luego, identifica la idea principal y escribe dos detalles de soporte. Escríbelos en el organizador el gráfico a continuación.

Tiger was the funniest cat we have ever had. He was the first cat to start drinking from our fish aquarium. I would laugh so hard every time I saw Tiger perched up on the fish aquarium, lapping up water from the water filter system! He never bothered the fish; he just loved to drink their water! Another funny thing that Tiger did was drink from the dog's bath water. Whenever we would be giving the dog a bath, Tiger would waltz over and start lapping up water from the tub. I don't think the dog appreciated that, but we sure thought it was funny! Tiger was definitely a very funny cat.

Main Idea

Supporting Detail

Supporting Detail

Food Fractions

Directions: Solve these fraction word problems.

Instrucciones: Resuelve estos problemas verbales de fracciones.

Example: Three girls bought a chocolate cake. Joanna ate $\frac{1}{4}$ of the cake. Michelle ate $\frac{3}{8}$ of the cake. How much was left for Sara?

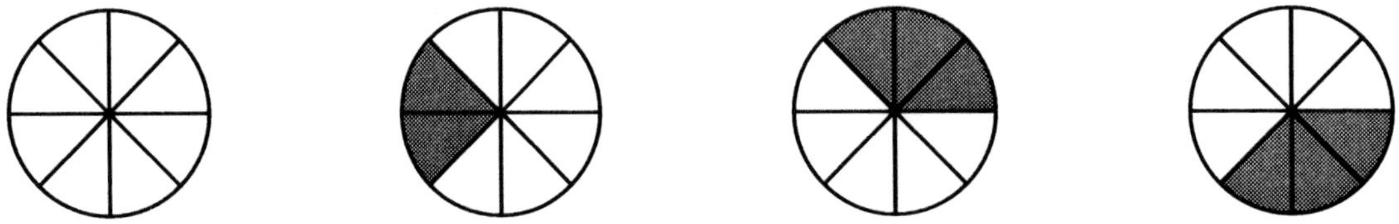

one whole cake $= \frac{8}{8}$

Joanna ate $\frac{1}{4}$ of the cake. $(\frac{2}{8} = \frac{1}{4})$

Michelle ate $\frac{3}{8}$ of the cake.

$\frac{3}{8}$ of the cake was left for Sara.

1. Susan and Julie bought a ham and pineapple pizza. Susan ate $\frac{3}{7}$ of the pizza.

   How much was left for Julie? ____________

2. Your best friend and you go to Pie Palace for pie. You eat $\frac{5}{6}$ of the pie.

   How much pie is left for your friend? ____________

3. Coach Joe bought a chocolate cake to share with the team. Coach Joe ate $\frac{7}{10}$ of the cake.

   How much cake was left for the team? ____________

4. Your dad bought one whole vegetarian pizza from Pizza Paradise. Your sister ate $\frac{5}{8}$ of the pizza before you got home.

   How much pizza was left for you? ____________

5. James and Ralph bought a pumpkin pie. James ate $\frac{2}{3}$ of the pie.

   How much pie was left for Ralph? ____________

Silly Stories

Directions: Choose one of the following story starters, then write a silly story.

Instrucciones: Elije una de las siguientes formas para comenzar los cuentos, luego escribe un cuento tonto.

#1	Katie lay in bed staring at the water stain right over her head on the ceiling. It was shaped like a key, and she often imagined it was a map of a different country.
#2	"Look!" Jake pointed a finger at the light flickering through the trees beyond the cabin window. Colin didn't answer. Instead, he covered his head with his sleeping bag.
#3	Once upon a time, there was a princess who lived in a castle by the sea. She could not speak, but everyone enjoyed her sweet smile and kind deeds.
#4	Silently, I walked up to the edge of the crowd. The people were watching some activity in the middle of the courtyard. I stood on my toes and tried to see over the heads of those standing in front of me.

I chose story starter #______.

At the Beach

Directions: Read each word. Replace the first one or two letters to make a new word related to something you might see at a beach. Use the letters from the Letter Box to help you. Cross out each one you use. The first one is done for you.

Instrucciones: Lee cada palabra. Reemplaza las primeras una o dos letras para formar una nueva palabra relacionada con algo que podrías ver en una playa. Usa las "Letters Box" para ayudarte. Tacha cada una, una vez que la uses. El primer ejemplo es para ti.

Letters Box

~~b~~
f
fl
g
k
l
s
sh
sp
sw
t
w

1. teach b e a c h
2. boggles _____ _____ _____ _____ _____ _____ _____
3. trim _____ _____ _____ _____
4. bloat _____ _____ _____ _____ _____
5. hand _____ _____ _____ _____
6. saves _____ _____ _____ _____ _____
7. bells _____ _____ _____ _____ _____ _____
8. dowel _____ _____ _____ _____ _____
9. flash _____ _____ _____ _____ _____ _____
10. skippers _____ _____ _____ _____ _____ _____ _____ _____
11. potion _____ _____ _____ _____ _____ _____
12. bites _____ _____ _____ _____ _____

The Most People

Directions: In the word search below, find and circle the names of the world's most populated countries. The names of the countries can be found going across, down, backwards, or diagonally in the puzzle.

Instrucciones: En la búsqueda de palabras a continuación, busca y encierra en un círculo los nombres de los lugares más poblados del mundo. Los nombres de los países se pueden encontrar cruzados, abajo, al revés o en diagonal en el rompecabezas.

More than half of all of the people in the world live in one of these 15 countries:

BANGLADESH	EGYPT	INDONESIA	NIGERIA	RUSSIA
BRAZIL	ETHIOPIA	JAPAN	PAKISTAN	UNITED STATES
CHINA	INDIA	MEXICO	PHILIPPINES	VIETNAM

C	B	H	I	V	J	A	P	A	N	N	A
N	A	T	S	I	K	A	P	I	N	D	I
U	N	I	T	E	D	S	T	A	T	E	S
A	G	C	D	T	M	E	X	I	C	O	U
B	L	H	I	N	D	O	N	E	S	I	A
R	A	I	N	A	I	S	S	U	R	I	E
A	D	N	T	M	E	D	S	T	A	T	G
Z	E	A	N	I	G	E	R	I	A	E	Y
I	S	E	N	I	P	P	I	L	I	H	P
L	H	S	E	T	H	I	O	P	I	A	T

What Do You See?

Once you have completed the puzzle, look closely at it. Put the letters that are **not circled** in order in the boxes below to answer the final question.

Final Question: Which three countries have the most people living in them?

1. ☐☐☐☐☐
2. ☐☐☐☐☐
3. ☐☐☐☐☐☐ ☐☐☐☐☐☐

Go Figure

Directions: Read each problem. Then, circle or write your answers. Show your work on #1, #3, and #4.

Instrucciones: Lee cada problema. Luego, encierra en un círculo o escribe tus respuestas. Muestra tu trabajo en los números 1, 3, y 4.

1. Sarah is climbing a mountain that is 1,905 feet high. She has already climbed 489 feet. How many more feet does Sarah still need to climb in order to make it to the top?

a. 2,394 ft. b. 1,584 ft. c. 1,416 ft. d. 584 ft.

2. Lee has 54 tools that he needs to separate into 6 piles. Which of the problems shown below would Lee use to find out how many tools need to be in each pile?

a. $54 \times 6 =$ b. $54 \div 6 =$ c. $54 - 6 =$ d. $54 + 6 =$

3. Jennie has 160 stuffed bears in her collection. She is storing her collection of bears in containers that hold 20 stuffed bears each. So far, she has already filled 5 containers. How many stuffed bears have NOT yet been put in a container for storage?

_______________ stuffed bears

4. There were 76 birds on the playground at Dawson Elementary. Then, 58 birds flew away. Ten minutes later, another 19 joined the remaining birds. How many birds are now on the playground?

_______________ birds

In Tense

What to Know

Verbs are an important part of sentences. Verbs may say what the subject does/did, or it may tell about the subject. Verbs can also tell us when something happens. If we want to change the time (tense) of a sentence, we need to change the form of the verb.

Examples: Josie **wears** sunscreen. (present tense)
Josie **wore** sunscreen. (past tense)
Josie **will wear** sunscreen. (future tense)

Directions: These sentences are all written in different tenses. Name the tenses.

Instrucciones: Estas oraciones están escritas en diferentes tiempos de verbales. Nombra los tiempos de verbo.

1. Yuki swims every day. ________________ tense
2. This summer will be very hot. ________________ tense
3. The sun burned the tips of my cat's ears. ________________ tense
4. Jack builds sandcastles at the beach. ________________ tense
5. I went to the beach last weekend. ________________ tense

Directions: These sentences are all written in the present tense. Rewrite them in the past tense by changing their verbs.

Instrucciones: Estas oraciones están todas escritas en tiempo presente. Vuelve a escribirlas en el pasado, cambiando los verbos.

6. Maria always wears a T-shirt over her bathing suit in the pool.

____

____

7. We pitch a tent for shade when we go on a picnic.

____

____

8. The day is hot and bright, so we wear hats and sunscreen.

____

____

Real-World Math

Directions: Read each problem. Then, circle or write your answers on the lines. Show your work.

Instrucciones: Lee cada problema. Luego, encierra en un círculo o escribe tus respuestas en las líneas. Muestra tu trabajo.

1. Howard made 3 flower beds in his backyard. They do not touch each other. Each flower bed is in the shape of an octagon. How many total sides are on all 3 flower beds?

_____________ sides

2. Wanda is making dough for kolaches that she is baking for a party. Wanda needs 2 tablespoons of salt for every 5 pounds of dough. Wanda is making 15 pounds of kolache dough. How many tablespoons of salt does she need?

   a. 2 tablespoons

   b. 4 tablespoons

   c. 6 tablespoons

   d. 10 tablespoons

3. When Jason left for work, the temperature was 32°F. By lunchtime, the temperature had risen 18 degrees. What was the temperature at lunchtime?

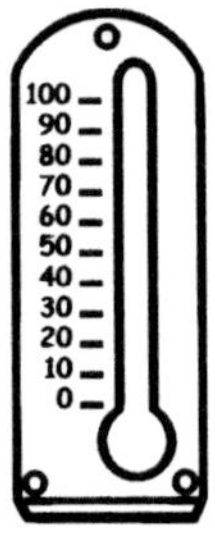

_____________ °F

4. Jim is putting holiday lights around the greenhouse in his yard. The greenhouse is in the shape of a rectangle that measures 6 feet wide and 8 feet long. How many feet of holiday lights will Jim need to complete this task?

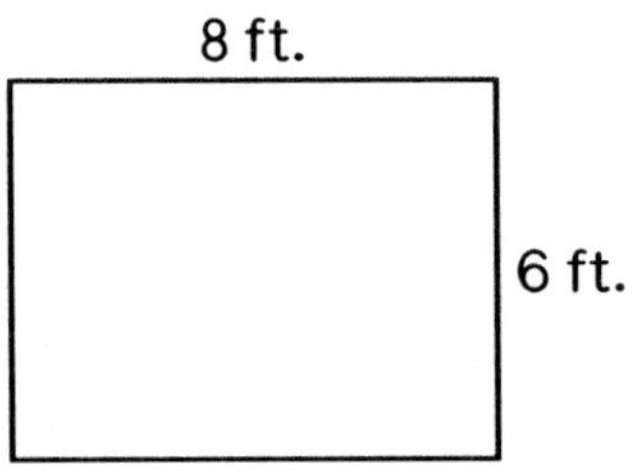

_____________ ft.

Sneeze Soup

Directions: Read the story, then circle the correct answers below.

Instrucciones: Lee el cuento, luego encierra en un círculo las respuestas correctas a continuación.

"The recipe calls for two tablespoons of pepper," said Dillon.

"Are you sure that's right?" asked Miranda. "I thought it was two teaspoons."

"Yep, it's right. Remember, this is special soup to help Mom feel better."

Miranda dumped the two tablespoons of pepper in and stirred the broth.

Miranda sniffed the soup and began sneezing. "Whew! That's a lot of pepper."

"It's going to be great," assured Dillon.

The soup simmered for 15 minutes. Dillon grabbed a soup bowl and began ladling the soup.

"Here we come, Mom," called Dillon, as he and Miranda brought the soup on a tray.

"Achoo!" said Mom. "What's this?"

"It's homemade soup, just for you. It's going to work better than medicine."

Mom took a big sniff of the soup in her lap and immediately started sneezing. She couldn't stop.

"Oh, no! It has too much pepper!" exclaimed Miranda.

"It's okay," interrupted Mom. "It's clearing my sinuses. How much pepper is in there?"

"Two tablespoons," said Dillon.

"I told you the recipe called for two TEASPOONS!" shouted Miranda.

1. Which of the following statements is *not* true?
   a. Miranda told Dillon to add two tablespoons of pepper.
   b. Mom was a good sport and made her kids feel good about helping her.
   c. Miranda was frustrated that there was too much pepper in the soup.
   d. Miranda trusted Dillon's instructions at the beginning of the passage.

2. What conclusions can be drawn about Miranda and Dillon's mom?
   a. She is an emotional person and cries a lot.
   b. She is supportive and understanding.
   c. She will probably never eat soup again.
   d. She tries to take over every situation.

3. After reading the passage, which of the following helps you answer the previous question?
   a. "How much pepper is in there?"
   b. "It's okay . . . It's clearing my sinuses."
   c. Mom took a big sniff of the soup.
   d. She couldn't stop sneezing.

Factor It Out

Directions: Fill in the missing factors in each row.

Instrucciones: Completa los factores que faltan en cada fila.

Row 1	9 × ______ = 54	3 × ______ = 36	10 × ______ = 60
Row 2	8 × ______ = 64	9 × ______ = 81	6 × ______ = 72
Row 3	______ × 5 = 45	______ × 12 = 48	______ × 7 = 42
Row 4	______ × 7 = 63	______ × 9 = 63	______ × 11 = 55
Row 5	6 × ______ = 36	9 × ______ = 36	8 × ______ = 56
Row 6	______ × 9 = 63	______ × 8 = 72	______ × 7 = 49
Row 7	42 ÷ 7 = ______	36 ÷ 4 = ______	32 ÷ 8 = ______
Row 8	27 ÷ 3 = ______	72 ÷ 9 = ______	48 ÷ 8 = ______

Combine and Improve

What to Know One way to improve the quality of your paragraphs is to combine short, simple sentences.

Example: Jarrod was beside us. Jake was beside us. We did not know they were even in the house.

Jarrod and Jake were beside us before we knew they were even in the house.

What to Know Another way to make your sentences more interesting is to move around the parts of your sentences so they do not always start the same way—with the subject, for example.

Example: Before we knew they were even in the house, Jarrod and Jake were beside us.

Directions: Improve the sentences in the following paragraph by combining short, simple ones and by moving around the parts of the sentences so they do not always start the same way. Rewrite the improved paragraph.

Instrucciones: Mejora las oraciones en el siguiente párrafo combinando oraciones cortas y simples, y moviendo las partes de las oraciones para que no siempre comiencen de la misma manera. Vuelve a escribir el párrafo mejorado.

Trees Bear Gifts

Trees give us many things. Trees give us shade on hot days. Trees give us wood with which to build our homes. Trees give us fruit to eat. Trees give us leaves we can use for mulch. Trees provide shelter for the birds and other animals we enjoy. Trees give shelter from the rain. Trees can be good places to hide. Trees can be good places to play. Trees give us a place to build tree houses. Trees are also beautiful to look at. Trees may stay green all year long. Trees may lose all their leaves in the fall and winter. Trees may produce flowers.

It Adds Up

Directions: Use the prices to write addition problems. Find the sums.

Instrucciones: Usa los precios para escribir problemas de suma. Encuentra las sumas.

1.

______ + ______ = ______

2.

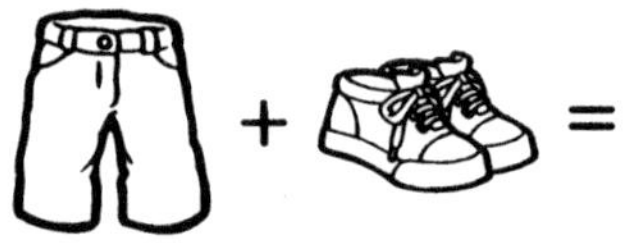

______ + ______ = ______

3.

______ + ______ = ______

4.

______ + ______ + ______ = ______

5.

______ + ______ = ______

6.

______ + ______ + ______ = ______

A Sports Story

Directions: Read the following story, then number the events in the order in which they occurred. One has been done for you.

Instrucciones: Lee el cuento siguiente, luego enumera los eventos en el orden en que ocurrieron. La primera se encuentra dada.

Eddie has always been into sports. Before playing basketball, he played soccer. His soccer team went to the state championships and won a trophy when he was in the fifth grade. It was a very exciting game, and Eddie scored the winning goal!

Now, Eddie plays basketball on the ninth-grade basketball team. Next year, he will try out for the tenth-grade soccer team as well. Then, he will be playing team sports practically all year round. When Eddie was five years old, his big sister took him to a college soccer game, and that's when he decided that he wanted to play on a sports team.

Today, his sister Jessica comes to his basketball games and claims that she inspired him to be the great athlete that he is. Eddie just laughs when she says that, but he does agree that she had a part in his love for athletics. Jessica frequently tells him that if he works hard, he can do anything. Eddie's most recent dream is to go to college on a basketball scholarship and study physics.

4th 1. Eddie plays on the ninth-grade basketball team.

_____ 2. Eddie decided that he wanted to play on a sports team.

_____ 3. Eddie's fifth-grade soccer team won the state championships.

_____ 4. Eddie will go to college and study physics.

_____ 5. Eddie scored the winning goal for his fifth-grade soccer team.

_____ 6. Eddie will try out for the tenth-grade soccer team.

Whose House?

Directions: Read each clue to fill in the chart below. If the answer to the clue is "yes," make a ✓ in the box. If the answer is "no," make an X in the box. Then, answer the statements below the chart.

Instrucciones: Lea cada clave para completar el cuadro a continuación. Si la respuesta a la clave es *sí*, haz una ✓en el cuadro. Si la respuesta es *no*, marca con una X en la casilla. Luego, contesta las afirmaciones debajo del cuadro.

Clues

- Marie's house number has only odd digits in it.
- Jay's house number has more even digits than odd digits.
- Sean's house number is evenly divisible by 3.
- Larissa's house number is evenly divisible by 10.

	61	476	810	954	977
Jay					
Tina					
Larissa					
Sean					
Marie					

1. Jay's house number is __________.
2. Tina's house number is __________.
3. Larissa's house number is _______.
4. Sean's house number is __________.
5. Marie's house number is __________.

Paragraph Maze

Directions: Find your way through the maze by making a paragraph. Some words in the paragraph are written right to left and bottom to top, so read carefully!

Instrucciones: Encuentra tu camino a través del laberinto haciendo un párrafo. Algunas palabras en el párrafo están escritas de derecha a izquierda y de abajo hacia arriba, ¡léelas con atención!

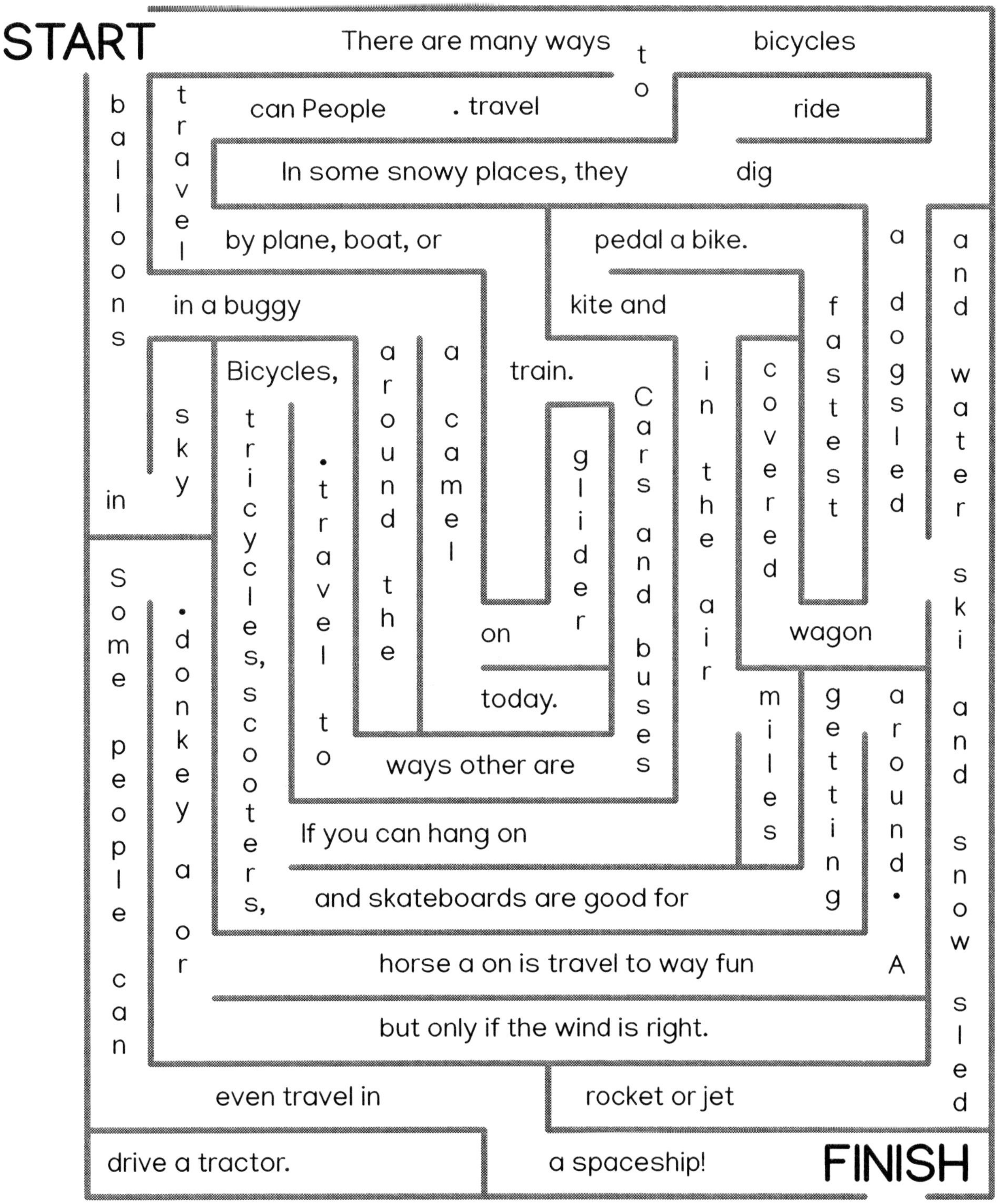

Two Graphs

Directions: Answer the questions based on the pie chart about books.

Instrucciones: Responde las preguntas según el gráfico circular sobre libros.

Types of Books Bought

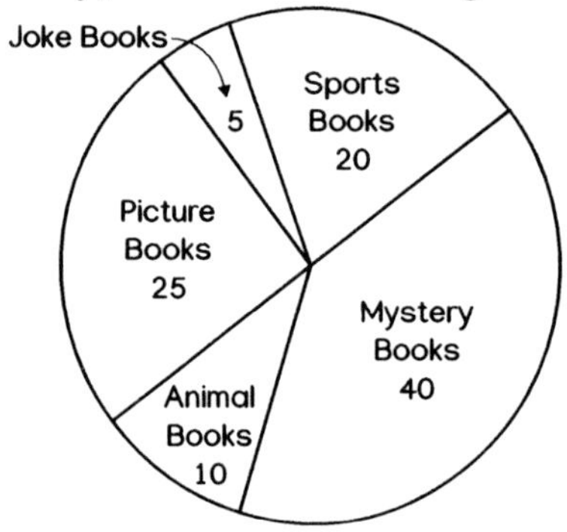

1. How many books were bought in all?

   ____

2. Which type of book was bought more than picture books?

   ____

3. How many more mystery books were bought than animal books?

   ____

4. Which type of book was bought the least?

   ____

   Which type of book was bought the most?

   ____

Directions: Answer the questions based on the pictograph about ice cream.

Instrucciones: Responde las preguntas basadas en el pictograma sobre el helado.

5. How many chocolate ice cream cones were sold?

   ____

6. Which flavor of ice cream cone sold the most?

   ____

7. How many more strawberry cones were sold than vanilla cones?

   ____

8. How many ice cream cones were sold in all?

   ____

Ice Cream Cones Sold on Sunday

Story Detective

Directions: The following story gives you many clues about what Daryl and his family are planning to do. Read the story carefully, then answer the questions below.

Instrucciones: El cuento siguiente te da muchas pistas sobre lo que Daryl y su familia están planeando hacer. Lee el cuento con cuidado, luego, responde las preguntas a continuación.

Daryl couldn't believe the day was finally here! His mother woke him up early and rushed him to breakfast. "Make sure you wash your own bowl and put it back, Daryl," his mother said, "I don't want dirty dishes left behind." Daryl reached into a box filled with newspaper-wrapped dishes and pulled out a bowl for his breakfast.

As Daryl finished washing his dish, his best friend, Larry, came to the back door. "Hey, Daryl! I thought I'd better bring this sweatshirt over to you," he explained. "You left it at my house a while back. It might be some time before I see you again."

"Thanks," Daryl replied with a smile. "I wondered what happened to that."

"Yeah, and you're probably going to really need it now," Larry stated. "No more beach clothes for you!"

"Yeah," said Daryl, "but I'm ready for a change."

1. What can you infer from this story? What are Daryl and his family getting ready to do? (Be as specific as you can.)

____

____

____

2. What clues helped you to make this inference? List at least three specific clues from the story.

____

____

____

____

Money Math

Directions: Solve each problem. The first one is done for you.

Instrucciones: Resuelve cada problema. El primer ejemplo es para ti.

1.
$$\begin{array}{r} \$4.20 \\ +\$3.99 \\ \hline \$8.19 \end{array}$$

2.
$$\begin{array}{r} \$28.99 \\ +\$41.35 \\ \hline \end{array}$$

3.
$$\begin{array}{r} \$10.50 \\ -\$\ \ 5.42 \\ \hline \end{array}$$

4.
$$\begin{array}{r} \$58.14 \\ -\$26.25 \\ \hline \end{array}$$

5.
$$\begin{array}{r} \$39.73 \\ +\$17.41 \\ \hline \end{array}$$

6.
$$\begin{array}{r} \$4.87 \\ +\$1.87 \\ \hline \end{array}$$

7.
$$\begin{array}{r} \$10.23 \\ +\$\ \ 7.64 \\ \hline \end{array}$$

8.
$$\begin{array}{r} \$6.20 \\ -\$1.11 \\ \hline \end{array}$$

9.
$$\begin{array}{r} \$8.23 \\ -\$2.50 \\ \hline \end{array}$$

10. Mrs. Mayberry bought pencils for \$3.18, and Mrs. Penn bought notebooks for \$8.76. How much money did they spend in all?

____

What's a Subject?

What to Know

A **sentence** is a group of words that tell about something. A sentence tells about a person, place, thing, or idea. A **subject** of a sentence is who or what the sentence is about.

Example: The boy ran.

Who is this sentence about? This sentence is about the boy.
The subject of this sentence is *the boy*.

(The boy) (ran.)

Who or what? — What happened?

Directions: Read the following sentences and look for the subject of each one. Who or what is the sentence about? Circle the subject in each sentence.

Instrucciones: Lee las siguientes oraciones y busca el sujeto de cada una. ¿De quién o de qué se trata la oración? Haz un círculo en cada oración.

1. The school was given the top rating.
2. The dog is attending obedience school.
3. The sun set on the horizon.
4. Fourth graders love to read.
5. Spring is coming.

Directions: Look at the subjects below. Write sentences using each of these subjects. Remember, the sentences must be about these subjects.

Instrucciones: Mira los temas siguientes temas. Escribe oraciones usando cada uno de estos sujetos. Recuerda, las oraciones deben ser acerca de estos sujetos.

6. Lisa

____

7. zoo

____

8. peanuts

____

9. bicycle

____

10. airplane

____

Word Problems

Directions: Read each problem. Then, circle or write your answers on the lines. Show your work.

Instrucciones: Lee cada problema. Luego, haz un círculo o escribe tus respuestas sobre las líneas. Muestra tu trabajo.

1. Into how many groups of 5 can the stars shown here be divided?

   a. 2 with 5 left over

   b. 3 with 3 left over

   c. 4 with 2 left over

   d. 5 with 3 left over

2. Kane bought 3 boxes of candy. There were 12 candy bars in each box. Four of the twelve candy bars had peanuts, and the rest had caramel. Each box cost $4.90. How many candy bars did Kane buy?

_________________ candy bars

3. Lois charges $25 for each yard she mows. Over the summer, she mowed 63 yards. How much money did Lois earn?

$ _________________

4. Justin bought 8 cases of soda for his sister's party. There were 24 cans in each case. How many cans of soda did Justin buy altogether?

_________________ cans of soda

About Mozart

Directions: Read the story, then circle the correct answers below.

Instrucciones: Lee el cuento, luego haz un círculo alrededor de las respuestas correctas.

Mozart is one of the world's most famous composers. Mozart's music is so famous that it is listened to all over the world. How did Mozart come to write such beautiful music?

Mozart was born in Austria. He was the son of a well-known composer and teacher. Mozart received lessons from his father and was playing before royalty and other important people by the age of six. By the time he was 10 years old, Mozart had traveled and played music all over Europe.

It didn't take long for Mozart to begin writing music of his own. He wrote many musical works. Though his music was loved, Mozart was not paid for writing it. He received money only when he would play. He had to give piano lessons to earn enough money to live.

It wasn't until 1780 when Mozart was finally paid to write music. He was given the job to write an opera. He produced his most famous work in the next three years. When Mozart died in 1791, he left a legacy of beautiful music that would impress crowds all over the world.

1. What is the author's main purpose for writing this passage about Mozart?
   - a. to share the facts about Mozart's father
   - b. to share the inspiring story of Mozart
   - c. to point out that Mozart was not paid enough
   - d. to list all works written by Mozart

2. Which sentence from the passage shows how the author feels about Mozart?
   - a. He produced his most famous work in the next three years.
   - b. How did Mozart come to write such beautiful music?
   - c. He received money only when he would play.
   - d. By the time he was 10 years old, Mozart had traveled and played music all over Europe.

3. Which of the following statements **did not** happen?
   - a. Mozart learned to play beautiful music at a very young age.
   - b. Mozart was naturally talented and skilled.
   - c. Mozart was paid to play for the president of the United States.
   - d. Mozart left a legacy of music that is still played today.

Probability

Directions: Read each problem. Then, circle each correct answer.

Instrucciones: Lee cada problema, luego haz un círculo alrededor de las respuestas correctas.

1. Jake has a deck of cards with letters printed on them. He has 2 cards with an "A," 2 cards with a "B," 2 cards with a "C," and 3 cards with a "D." If he shuffles the cards and turns them over one at a time, what will the last card be?

D	B	D	C	A	D	B	C	

a. A **b.** B **c.** C **d.** D

2. Linda has 5 ink pens in her purse. Two are black, 1 is green, and 2 are red. Which of the following combinations is NOT possible if Linda chooses 3 ink pens from her purse?

a. 2 red and 1 green

b. 1 green and 2 blue

c. 2 black and 1 green

d. 2 red and 1 black

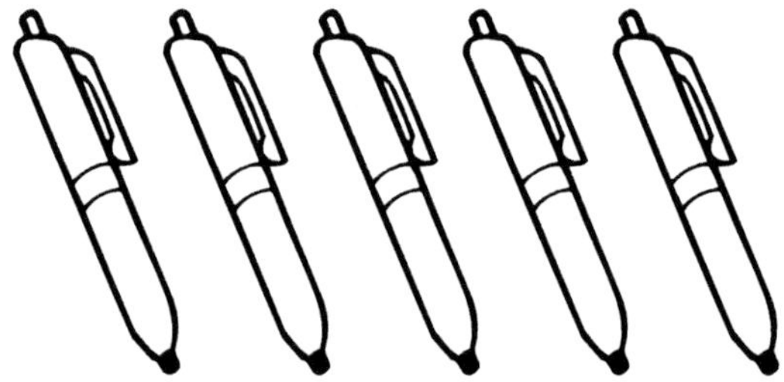

3. The table shows how many picture cards Jimmy has. Based on the table, what card will Jimmy turn over next?

Cat	2
Dog	3
Rabbit	2
Butterfly	2

a. butterfly **b.** dog **c.** cat **d.** rabbit

What's a Predicate?

What to Know

Just as all sentences have a subject, they also have a **predicate.** A predicate tells important things about the subject. The predicate tells what the subject does, has, or is.

In the sentence below, the word *ran* is the predicate.
It explains what *the boy*, the subject, is doing.

Directions: Draw a circle around the subject in each sentence below. Once you have located the subject in each of the sentences, underline the predicate.

Instrucciones: Dibuja un círculo alrededor del sujeto de cada una de las oraciones a continuación. Una vez que ubiques el sujeto en cada una de ellas, subraya el predicado.

1. The dog jumped into the lake.
2. Everyone was laughing.
3. Erika has a cold.
4. The cat jumped off the log.
5. They ate the birthday cake.
6. She can do a backward flip.
7. Summer is the time for fishing.

Directions: Write sentences using the following predicates.

Instrucciones: Escribe oraciones usando los predicados siguientes.

8. jumped into the water ____________________
9. claps at the end ____________________
10. eats hot dogs ____________________
11. races the boys ____________________
12. is happy ____________________
13. sits on the bench ____________________
14. always eats ketchup ____________________

Word Machines

Directions: Look at the letters in the grids below. How many words can you think of using the given letters? Follow the rules below to find the answers. Two examples of words are given for the first grid.

Instrucciones: Mira las letras en las cuadrículas de abajo. ¿Cuántas palabras se te ocurren usando las letras dadas? Sigue las siguientes reglas para encontrar las respuestas. Se dan dos ejemplos de palabras para la primera cuadrícula.

Rules

- You must use the central letter of the grid as the beginning letter of each word.
- No letter can be used more than the number of times it is given.
- Letters do not need to be connected.
- No proper nouns or slang words allowed.

1.

L	O	D
B	F	N
I	L	D

Words

fib
fill

2.

M	T	A
I	L	N
D	E	F

Words

3.

L	A	B
I	C	R
L	S	T

Words

Tricky Shapes

Directions: Look at the figure below. How many triangles are there? __________

Instrucciones: Mira la figura. ¿Cuántos triángulos hay?

Hint: Don't forget to look for the upside-down triangles or the ones you can make by combining triangles.

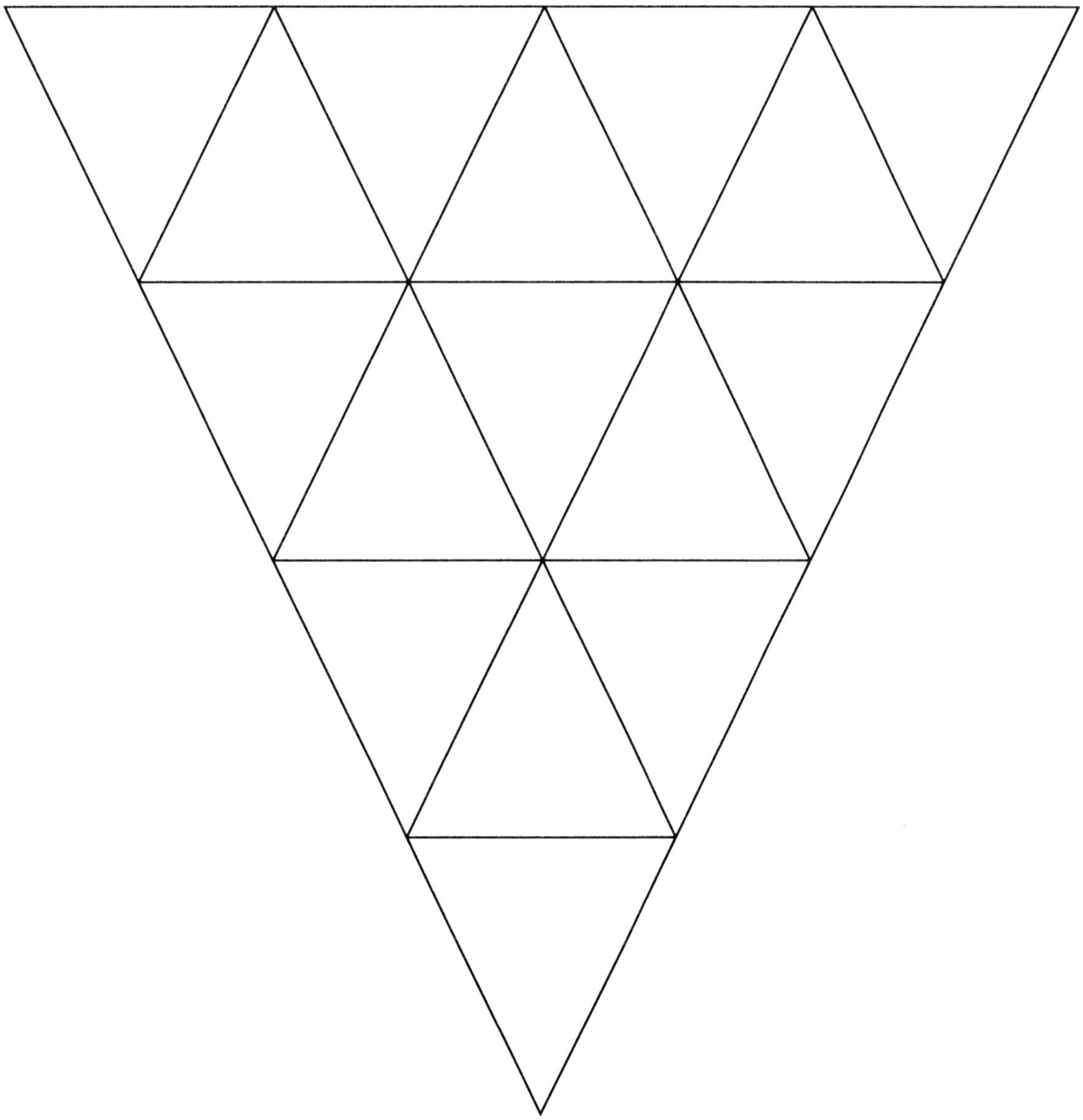

How many quadrilaterals are in the figure below? __________

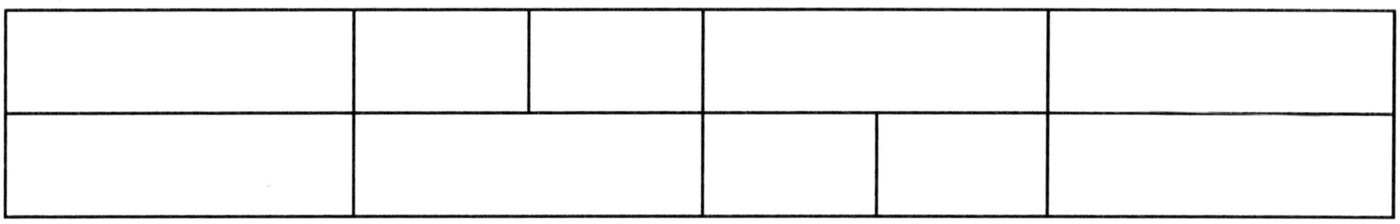

Divide and Conquer

Directions: Do these problems. The first two have been done for you.

Instrucciones: Resuelve estos problemas. Los primeros dos ejemplos son para ti.

1. 122 R5 $6\overline{)737}$ −6 13 −12 17 −12 5	2. 175 R2 $3\overline{)527}$ −3 22 −21 17 −15 2	3. $4\overline{)293}$	4. $4\overline{)531}$
5. $5\overline{)617}$	6. $2\overline{)193}$	7. $6\overline{)437}$	8. $8\overline{)293}$
9. $4\overline{)857}$	10. $6\overline{)273}$	11. $3\overline{)313}$	12. $7\overline{)629}$

Connecting Thoughts

What to Know

Segues (pronounced "seg-ways") and **transitions** are used to connect thoughts and ideas. The chart below contains a list of common segues and transitions.

Directions: As you read the following sentences, notice the segues and transitions used. Notice how they enhance the sentences. Also note the comma use in some of the sentences.

Instrucciones: Mientras lee las siguientes oraciones, observa las transiciones que se usan. Observa cómo se realzan las oraciones. También ten en cuenta el uso de la coma en algunas de las oraciones.

- Consequently, the director decided to "cut" the scene.
- Obviously, the students had practiced their instruments quite a bit.
- As a result of reading the first book, I knew what to expect.

Now, write your own sentences. In each sentence, use at least one segue or transition from the box below.

1. ______________________________
2. ______________________________
3. ______________________________
4. ______________________________
5. ______________________________

above	clearly	meanwhile
according to	consequently	moreover
additionally	even though	nevertheless
after	for instance	next
along with	furthermore	obviously
also	however	of course
although	in addition to	similarly
another	in conclusion	since
as a result	in fact	therefore
because	last	while
besides	lastly	yet

Find the Answer

Directions: Read each problem. Then, circle or write your answers on the lines.

Instrucciones: Lee cada problema. Luego, haz un círculo o escribe tus respuestas en las líneas.

1. What should you do to find the next number in the pattern?

188, 178, 168, 158, ______

- **a.** add 9 to 158
- **b.** add 10 to 158
- **c.** subtract 10 from 158
- **d.** subtract 10 from 188

2. Solve the problems below.

- **a.** $(10 \times 15) \div 5 =$ ______________
- **b.** $(8 \div 4) \times 3 =$ ______________
- **c.** $3 \times (15 \div 3) =$ ______________
- **d.** $(6 \times 6) \div 2 =$ ______________
- **e.** $(12 \div 4) \times 2 =$ ______________
- **f.** $3 \times (4 \div 4) =$ ______________

3. Dahlia folded her green, yellow, orange, and white T-shirts and placed them in her drawer. The green was on top of the white T-shirt. The orange was on top of all the other T-shirts. The yellow shirt was on top of the green shirt but under the orange shirt. List the order Dahlia placed her T-shirts in her drawer.

Top	
Bottom	

Always Growing

Directions: Read the nonfiction text in the box. Answer the questions below.

Instrucciones: Lee en texto de no ficción en el recuadro. Responde las preguntas a continuación.

Your body is changing and growing all of the time. But some parts of you grow faster than other parts. For example, your hair grows about half an inch each month. That means it grows about 6 inches per year.

Your fingernails and toenails also grow quickly. But did you know that not all of your fingernails grow at the same speed? The nails on your longer fingers actually grow faster than the nails on your shorter fingers. This means that the nails on your middle fingers grow the fastest. The next fastest are the nails on your ring fingers and your index fingers. The nails on your thumbs grow the slowest of all your fingernails. The time of year is also important, as your nails grow faster in the summertime than they do in the winter.

1. According to the text, about how many inches would your hair grow every four years? ____________________

2. According to the story, during which month would your fingernails grow the fastest? Circle your answer.

   March   July   October   December

3. Look at the picture of the hand. Put a **1** on the nail that grows the fastest. Put a **4** on the nail that grows the fourth fastest.

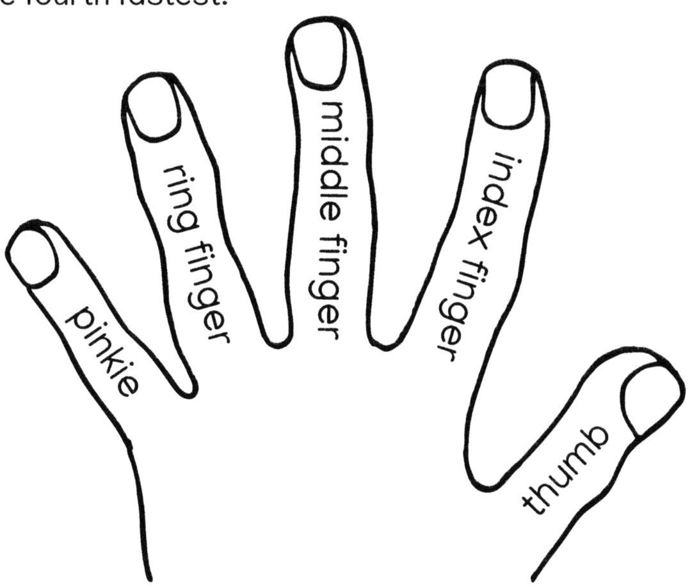

Averages

Directions: Calculate the average for each of the problems. The first one has been started for you. Show your work.

Instrucciones: Calcula el promedio para cada problema. El primer ejemplo es para ti. Muestra tu trabajo.

1. Shawna had 3 math grades: 80, 90, and 100. What was her average math grade?

$$\frac{80 + 90 + 100}{3} =$$

Her average math grade was __________.

2. James had 3 science grades: 60, 70, and 80. What was his average science grade?

His average science grade was ________.

3. Susan had 4 social studies grades: 93, 86, 70, and 71. What was her average social studies grade?

Her average social studies grade was __________.

4. The weights of 5 puppies were 12 pounds, 39 pounds, 15 pounds, 24 pounds, and 30 pounds. What was their average weight?

Their average weight was ______ pounds.

5. The weights of 5 rocks were 12 pounds, 48 pounds, 18 pounds, 32 pounds, and 35 pounds. What was the average weight?

The average weight was ______ pounds.

6. In the zoo, the weights of 6 bear cubs were 77 pounds, 104 pounds, 99 pounds, 97 pounds, 88 pounds, and 63 pounds. What was their average weight?

Their average weight was ______ pounds.

What's the Question?

Directions: Write a question for each of the following answers. The first one has been done for you.

Instrucciones: Escribe una pregunta para cada una de las siguientes respuestas. El primer ejemplo es para ti.

1. **Question:** What natural occurrence happens when the ground shakes?

   Answer: an earthquake

2. **Question:** ____________________

   Answer: the giraffe and the zebra

3. **Question:** ____________________

   Answer: $1,349.90

4. **Question:** ____________________

   Answer: London, England

5. **Question:** ____________________

   Answer: apricots, apples, and apes

6. **Question:** ____________________

   Answer: a marathon

7. **Question:** ____________________

   Answer: Mona Lisa

8. **Question:** ____________________

   Answer: a turtle

Round and Solve

Directions: For problems 1–4, round to the nearest 10. For problems 5–8, round to the nearest 100. For problems 9–10, solve the problems and show your work.

Instrucciones: Para los problemas 1–4, redondea al 10 más cercano. Para los problemas 5–8, redondea al 100 más cercano. Para los problemas 9–10, resuelve los problemas y muestra tu trabajo.

1. 42 ____________

2. 78 ____________

3. 56 ____________

4. 186 ____________

5. 5,329 ____________

6. 864 ____________

7. 729 ____________

8. 671 ____________

9. Daniel saw 16 trees, 12 bushes, 23 flowers, and 2 lizards on his walk in the woods. How many things did Daniel see altogether?

____

10. Greta is 6 years younger than her brother. Her brother is 13. How old is Greta?

____

Given a Chance

Directions: Find the meaning of each underlined word in the story. Using the Definitions Box, put the letter of the answer on the blank line.

Instrucciones: Encuentra el significado de cada palabra subrayada en el cuento. Utilizando el "Definitions Box", pon la letra de la respuesta en la línea en blanco.

Definitions Box		
	a. to give pay in exchange for work	d. voted in, chosen
	b. a member of a group or squad	e. something that stops or restricts
	c. needed	

1. ______
2. ______
3. ______
4. ______
5. ______

Marion Motley just wanted a chance to do what he did best: play football. Marion Motley was an African American, and for a long time, no professional football teams wanted to [1]employ African Americans. Finally, at the age of 26, Motley was given a chance to try out for one team, the Cleveland Browns. The year was 1946—one year before Jackie Robinson broke the color [2]barrier in baseball. Motley made the team, and he went on to be one of the greatest players in football history. He was a big, fast, tough runner who led the league in rushing in 1948 and 1950. He was also a great blocker who risked getting hurt in order to protect his team's quarterback. This was one of the reasons why Motley was known as a great [3]teammate; he would do whatever was [4]necessary to help his team win. And the Browns won a lot! From 1946-1950, the Browns won five straight championships. In 1968, Motley became the second African American to be [5]elected to the Pro Football Hall of Fame.

Directions: Are the following pairs synonyms (same meaning) or antonyms (opposite meaning)? Write **S** (for synonym) or **A** (for antonym).

Instrucciones: ¿Son los siguientes pares sinónimos (mismo significado) o antónimos (significado opuesto)? Escribe **S** (para sinónimo) o **A** (para antónimo).

6. employ	hire	______
7. barrier	opening	______
8. teammate	enemy	______
9. necessary	required	______
10. elected	refused	______

Who Plays What?

Directions: Do you participate on a sports team? The six children in this chart each compete in a different sport. From the clues below, determine the sport that each child plays. Mark the correct boxes with a **Y** for *yes* and the incorrect boxes with an **N** for *no*.

Instrucciones: ¿Participas en algún equipo deportivo? Los seis niños en este cuadro compiten cada uno en un deporte diferente. A partir de las siguientes claves, determina el deporte que practica cada niño. Marca las casillas correctas con una **Y** para *sí* ("yes") y las casillas incorrectas con una **N** para *no*.

	Soccer	Basketball	Volleyball	Baseball	Swimming	Track
Anne						
Elise						
Ethan						
Katie						
Kevin						
Logan						

Clues

- Ethan needs water to compete.
- Anne's sport requires knee pads.
- Elise dribbles a ball with her hands.
- Katie's sport begins and ends with the same letters as Elise's sport.
- Logan is a goalie.
- Kevin runs in circles.

Set A and Set B

Directions: Complete the page after evaluating the examples below.

Instrucciones: Completa la página después de evaluar los ejemplos a continuación.

These figures have something in common. They all belong to Set A.

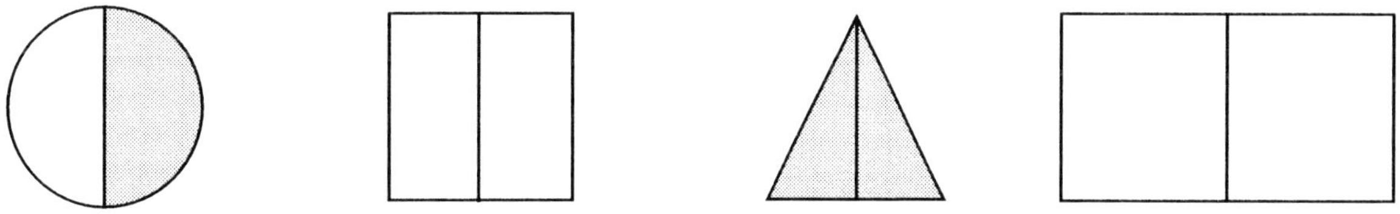

None of these figures can belong to Set A.

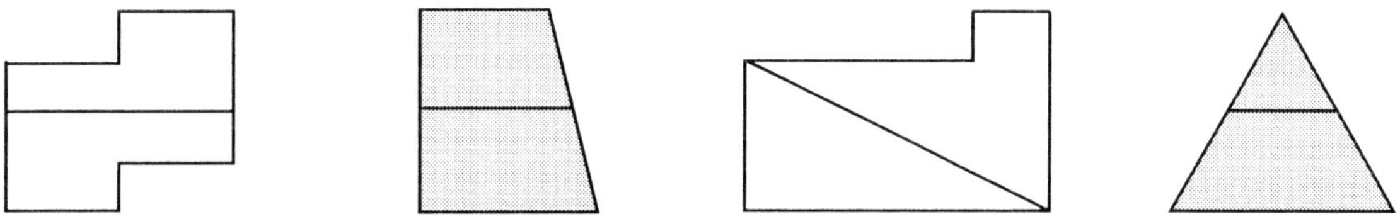

1. What makes something belong to Set A? According to your answer, draw another figure that would belong to Set A.

   Answer: ______________________________

   ____

These figures have something in common. They all belong to Set B.

None of these figures can belong to Set B.

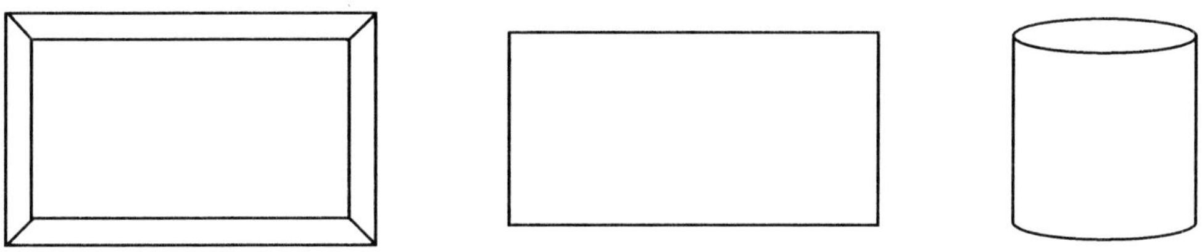

2. What makes something belong to Set B? According to your answer, draw another figure that would belong to Set B.

   Answer: ______________________________

   ____

Terms and More

Directions: For problems 1–8, circle the correct term for the underlined part of each number sentence. Then, solve problem 9.

Instrucciones: Para los problemas 1 a 8, haz un círculo alrededor del término correcto para la parte subrayada de cada oración numerica. Luego, resuelve el problema 9.

1. $\underline{81} \div 9 = 9$
   - a. minuend
   - b. addend
   - c. multiplier
   - d. dividend

2. $\underline{6} \times 6 = 36$
   - a. subtrahend
   - b. addend
   - c. multiplier
   - d. dividend

3. $\underline{33} - 11 = 22$
   - a. minuend
   - b. addend
   - c. multiplier
   - d. dividend

4. $\underline{10 + 10} = 20$
   - a. subtrahends
   - b. addends
   - c. multipliers
   - d. divisors

5. $3 \times 5 = \underline{15}$
   - a. product
   - b. sum
   - c. difference
   - d. quotient

6. $10 - 8 = \underline{2}$
   - a. product
   - b. sum
   - c. difference
   - d. quotient

7. $23 + 23 = \underline{46}$
   - a. product
   - b. sum
   - c. difference
   - d. quotient

8. $20 \div 5 = \underline{4}$
   - a. product
   - b. sum
   - c. difference
   - d. quotient

9. It takes 24 inches of string to wrap a package. How much string will be needed to wrap 25 packages?

Show Your Work Here

____

Get a Clue

Directions: Read the story. Answer each question below by circling **Yes** or **No.** For each answer you give, state one clue from the story that helped you answer the question. The first one is done for you.

Instrucciones: Lee el cuento. Responde cada pregunta a continuación marcando con un círculo **Yes** o **No.** Para cada respuesta que das, indica una clave de la historia que te ayudó a responder la pregunta. El primer ejemplo es para ti.

At 8:25, Johnny rushed into the room. It was exactly 10 minutes after the bell rang. His hair stuck out in all directions, his heavy coat was mis-buttoned, and he was wearing fuzzy slippers. Mrs. Maddox rolled her eyes and said, "Again, Johnny? Maybe it's time to get a new alarm clock."

1. *Question:* Does this story take place in Johnny's house? Yes (No)

   Clue from the story: A bell rings, and the adult is called Mrs. Maddox so she is probably a teacher.

2. *Question:* Did the bell to begin the class ring at 8:15? Yes No

   Clue from the story: ______________________________

3. *Question:* Did Johnny spend a lot of time getting ready for school? Yes No

   Clue from the story: ______________________________

4. *Question:* Is the weather most likely cold this morning? Yes No

   Clue from the story: ______________________________

5. *Question:* Is this the first time Johnny has been late? Yes No

   Clue from the story: ______________________________

Week 5
Tuesday
Math

Add Signs and Solve

Directions: Place the ÷ sign and the = sign in the squares so that each number sentence is correct.

Instrucciones: Coloca el signo ÷ y el signo = en los cuadrados para que cada oración numérica esté correcta.

1. 48 ☐ 6 ☐ 8	**2.** 100 ☐ 10 ☐ 10	**3.** 18 ☐ 2 ☐ 9
4. 55 ☐ 5 ☐ 11	**5.** 63 ☐ 9 ☐ 7	**6.** 14 ☐ 7 ☐ 2
7. 25 ☐ 5 ☐ 5	**8.** 56 ☐ 7 ☐ 8	**9.** 36 ☐ 12 ☐ 3

Directions: Place the division sign, the equal sign, and the answer in the correct order.

Instrucciones: Coloca el signo de división, el signo de igual y la respuesta en el orden correcto.

10. 42 ☐ 6 ☐ ______	**11.** 9 ☐ 3 ☐ ______	**12.** 21 ☐ 7 ☐ ______
13. 36 ☐ 6 ☐ ______	**14.** 10 ☐ 2 ☐ ______	**15.** 28 ☐ 4 ☐ ______
16. 45 ☐ 5 ☐ ______	**17.** 6 ☐ 6 ☐ ______	**18.** 32 ☐ 8 ☐ ______

Directions: Solve and watch out for any remainders.

Instrucciones: Resuelve y presta atención a cualquiera de los restos.

19. 28 ÷ 6 = ______ R ______	**20.** 8 ÷ 6 = ______ R ______	**21.** 28 ÷ 9 = ______ R ______
22. 17 ÷ 8 = ______ R ______	**23.** 14 ÷ 3 = ______ R ______	**24.** 15 ÷ 7 = ______ R ______

All About Capitals

Directions: The following sentences need capitalization. Underline each letter that should be changed to a capital three times, then write the capital letter above the underlined letter.

Instrucciones: Las siguientes oraciones necesitan mayúsculas. Subraya cada letra que debe ser cambiada a mayúscula tres veces, luego escribe la letra mayúscula sobre la letra subrayada.

I N Y S

Example: i went to new york on saturday.

1. when i went to the store, i saw my teacher, mrs. rose.
2. my family will go to disneyland in july.
3. i am reading old yeller this week.
4. my sister sarah says her favorite subject is spanish.
5. on wednesday, we will celebrate groundhog day.
6. my brother said that mom was a cheerleader at eastside high school.
7. in august, we're going to visit aunt mary in san francisco, california.
8. benji had a birthday, so we sang "happy birthday to you."
9. my friend rosa speaks spanish, and i speak english.
10. my neighbor julia is going to paris, france, next june.

What's the Difference?

Directions: Find the differences between the times. Estimate first, then find the actual answer.

Instrucciones: Encuentra las diferencias entre los tiempos. Estima primero, luego encuentra la respuesta real.

	Starting Time	Finishing Time	Estimate	Actual Answer
1.	9:30 a.m.	11:15 a.m.		
2.	10:09 a.m.	11:11 a.m.		
3.	7:45 a.m.	8:50 a.m.		
4.	9:00 a.m.	11:51 a.m.		
5.	3:35 p.m.	6:42 p.m.		
6.	8:25 p.m.	11:05 p.m.		
7.	1:07 a.m.	4:45 a.m.		
8.	8:00 a.m.	12:20 p.m.		

Directions: Estimate how long it takes to do the following things.

Instrucciones: Calcule cuánto tiempo se tarda en hacer las siguientes cosas.

9. brush your teeth ______________
10. travel to school ______________
11. tie your shoelaces ______________
12. pack your lunch ______________
13. eat lunch ______________
14. get dressed ______________
15. complete your homework ______________
16. sharpen your pencil ______________

Find the Causes

Directions: Read the story carefully. Follow the directions for each question, then answer the questions in complete sentences.

Instrucciones: Lee atentamente el cuento. Sigue las instrucciones para cada pregunta, luego responde las preguntas en oraciones completas.

It was a bright and sunny day when Jessica got into the car. She could not believe that her father was finally letting her drive his car. Jessica had gotten her driver's license a month ago, but her dad was very protective of his car and refused to let her drive it anywhere. Today, however, her father was in an especially happy mood and agreed that she could use his car for the afternoon. Now, Jessica was happily headed to her best friend Jacquie's house.

As Jessica pulled out of the driveway, her favorite song came on, so she turned up the volume of the radio. Just as she pulled onto the road, a dog ran out in the middle of the street. Jessica swerved to miss the dog and ended up running into the neighbors' trash cans. "Oh, no!" Jessica thought. "Now Dad will never let me drive his car again!"

1. Underline the sentence in the story that says Jessica's father agreed to let her use his car for the afternoon.

   What caused Jessica's father to let her drive his car for the afternoon? ______________

   ____

   ____

   ____

2. Underline the sentence in the story that says Jessica turned up the volume of the radio.

   What caused Jessica to turn up the volume of the radio? ______________

   ____

   ____

3. Underline the sentence in the story that says Jessica swerved the car.

   What caused Jessica to swerve? ______________

   ____

   ____

Decimals and Fractions

Directions: For problems 1–6, write each fraction as a decimal. For problems 7–8, write each decimal as a fraction. Then, solve problems 9–10. Show your work.

Instrucciones: Para los problemas 1 a 6, escribe cada fracción como un decimal. Para los problemas 7 y 8, escribe cada decimal como una fracción. Luego, resuelve los problemas 9 y 10. Muestra tu trabajo.

1. $\frac{6}{10}$ __________

2. $\frac{4}{10}$ __________

3. $\frac{9}{100}$ __________

4. forty-eight and seven hundredths __________

5. $2\frac{7}{10}$ __________

6. nine and three tenths __________

7. 0.7 __________

8. 0.2 __________

9. The Watsons had a pizza for supper. It was divided into 8 slices. Joey, his mom, and his dad each had $\frac{1}{4}$ of the pizza. How many slices did each person eat? __________

10. If you could only buy one shirt, and the price was two for $12.50, how much would one shirt cost? __________

More Cause and Effect

What to Know

Cause and **effect** explains why an event occurred by telling the results of an action.

Directions: List four possible causes for each of the following effects.

Instrucciones: Haz una lista de cuatro causas posibles para cada uno de los siguientes efectos.

Mrs. Hill's whole class got an extra hour of Friday Fun Time.

1. ____________________
2. ____________________
3. ____________________
4. ____________________

Several farm animals have wandered away from the farm.

1. ____________________
2. ____________________
3. ____________________
4. ____________________

Local police officers have closed a bridge.

1. ____________________
2. ____________________
3. ____________________
4. ____________________

A short boy is made captain of the basketball team.

1. ____________________
2. ____________________
3. ____________________
4. ____________________

Idiom Crossword

Directions: To complete the idiom, fill in the blanks with the words in the Word Bank. Then, use the missing words to complete the crossword puzzle.

Instrucciones: Para completar el modismo, llena los espacios en blanco con las palabras del "Word Bank". Entonces, usa las palabras que faltan para completar el siguiente crucigrama.

Word Bank

- bed
- bone
- ceiling
- crazy
- goat
- handle
- roof
- shoulder
- stack
- throat
- ~~warpath~~

Across

2. Have a ______________ to pick with you (to have an argument or try to settle a disagreement with someone)
4. Jump down your ______________ (to talk or scream at someone in an angry way)
6. Drive you ______________ (to annoy or irritate someone)
7. Get up on the wrong side of the ______________ (to get up in the morning in a bad mood)
8. Chip on your ______________ (not able to forgive)

Down

1. Get your ______________ (to annoy or irritate)
3. On the ______warpath______ (angry and upset)
5. Get a ______________ on something (to have control of something)
6. Hit the ______________ (to become very angry)
8. Blow your ______________ (to become very angry)
9. Go through the ______________ (to go very high or reach a high degree)

Weekend Jokes

Directions: Choose a word from the Word Bank below to complete each joke. Each word is used once. When you finish, try out your jokes on a friend.

Instrucciones: Elije una palabra del "Word Bank" a para completar cada chiste. Cada palabra es usada una sola vez. Cuando termines, prueba tus chistes con un amigo.

Word Bank				
	bring	hold	make	pay
	enjoy	keep	move	want

1. Tourist: "How do you ____________________ your workers?"

   Rancher: "with buffalo bills"

2. What can you ____________________ in your left hand but never in your right hand?

   Answer: your right elbow

3. When can an old horse ____________________ as fast as a speeding train?

   Answer: when it's on the train

4. What can you put in a sandbag to ____________________ it weigh less?

   Answer: a hole

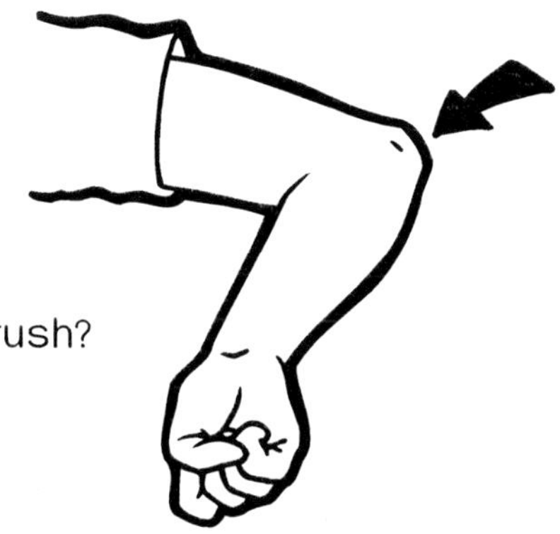

5. Why do ghosts ____________________ riding in elevators?

   Answer: It raises their spirits.

6. Which tool is the best to ____________________ to a gold rush?

   Answer: Take your pick.

7. Why do rabbits go on strike?

   Answer: They ____________________ a raise in celery.

8. How can you ____________________ your hair dry in the shower?

   Answer: Don't turn on the water.

Meters and Feet

Directions: Convert each measurement from meters to feet. Multiply the number of meters by 39 (inches), then divide that number by 12 to get the answer. Round each answer to the nearest foot.

Instrucciones: Convierte cada medida de metros a pies. Multiplica el número de metros por 39 (pulgadas), luego divide ese número por 12 para obtener la respuesta. Redondea cada respuesta al pie más cercano.

1. The first sprint in the 776 BCE Olympic Games was 192 meters long.

   192 meters = ____________________ feet

2. "World's Fastest Human" is the title given to the winner of the 100-meter sprint.

   100 meters = ____________________ feet

3. Male athletes run 110-meter hurdles.

   110 meters = ____________________ feet

4. A popular indoor race is 60 meters long.

   60 meters = ____________________ feet

5. The 1500-meter race is known as the metric mile. However, the measurement is not exactly a mile. Find the difference between a standard mile (5,280 feet) and a metric mile.

   1500 meters = ____________________ feet

   The difference between a metric mile and a standard mile is ____________________ feet.

Directions: Convert the measurements from feet to meters to the nearest hundredth. Multiply the number of feet by 12, then divide by 39 to get the answer.

Instrucciones: Convierte las medidas de pies a metros a la centésima más cercana. Multiplica el número de pies por 12, luego divide por 39 para obtener la respuesta.

6. Al Oerter, from the United States, was the first man to throw the discus more than 200 feet.

   200 feet = ____________________ meters

7. Sergei Bubka, from the Ukraine, was the first pole vaulter to clear 20 feet.

   20 feet = ____________________ meters

8. In 1990, Randy Barnes broke the standing outdoor shot put record with a throw of over 75 feet. His record lasted for 31 years.

   75 feet = ____________________ meters

Terrific Titles

Punctuation Rules

When punctuating titles, italicize or underline the titles of books, professional journals, plays, TV shows, movies, and magazines. For shorter works, such as articles, short stories, and poems, punctuate the titles with quotation marks.

Directions: Punctuate the titles correctly within the sentences.

Instrucciones: Coloca la puntuación de los títulos correctamente dentro de las oraciones.

1. I really enjoyed reading the book Chato and the Party Animals by Gary Soto.
2. One of the best poems I have ever read is Years Later by Lawrence Raab.
3. His little sister loves a TV show called Puppy Dog Pals.
4. I read an article entitled Dogs Are Man's Best Friend in a magazine recently.
5. We went to see the Broadway musical Wicked.
6. The book 20,000 Leagues Under the Sea by Jules Verne is packed with adventure.
7. In the movie Up, the main character ties balloons to his house and flies away.
8. This weekend, we went to see the play The Wizard of Oz.
9. Robert Frost wrote the poem The Road Not Taken.
10. In The Indian in the Cupboard series, Lynn Reid Banks stimulates the readers' imaginations.

Match and Expand

Directions: Expand these numbers. An example has been done for you.

Instrucciones: Expande estos números. El ejemplo es para ti.

Example: 2,641 = 2,000 + 600 + 40 + 1

1. 561 = ______________________________
2. 9,011 = ______________________________
3. 3,587 = ______________________________
4. 4,404 = ______________________________
5. 826 = ______________________________
6. 8,990 = ______________________________

Directions: Match the following numbers. The first one has been done for you.

Instrucciones: Relaciona los siguientes números. El primer ejemplo es para ti.

7. 3,659	(1 × 1,000) + (2 × 10) + (8 × 1)
8. 590	six one-hundreds
9. 1,028	800 + 70 + 5
10. 84	3 thousands + 5 hundreds + 15 tens + 9 ones
11. 600	no ones, no tens, three hundreds, two thousands
12. 2,300	seven ones, three tens, four hundreds, nine thousands
13. 875	nineteen hundreds, two ones
14. 9,437	five hundreds, eight tens, ten ones
15. 1,902	seven tens, fourteen ones

Directions: Write these numbers in standard form. Be careful of the place values!

Instrucciones: Escribe estas números en forma estándar.

16. 10 + 1,000 + 300 + 6 = ____________________
17. 400 + 4,000 + 6 = ____________________
18. 6 + 800 + 40 = ____________________

The Real Meaning

What to Know **Personification** is a figure of speech that portrays an animal, object, or idea as if it had human qualities.

Directions: Read each sentence. Underline the personification, then circle the answer that best gives the real meaning of this figure of speech. The first one has been done for you.

Instrucciones: Lee cada oración. Subraya la personificación, luego haz un círculo alrededor de la respuesta que mejor da el significado real de esta figura retórica. El primer ejemplo es para ti.

1. An old jalopy gagged and wheezed as it tried to climb the steep hill.
   - a. The car's driver was choking.
   - b. The car has run over something in the road.
   - c. The car's motor is making a lot of noise.
2. Curiosity ate away at Denise until she finally asked if the winning ticket was hers.
   - a. Denise has a terrible skin disease.
   - b. Denise could not stop thinking about her ticket.
   - c. Denise was being chewed upon by an animal.
3. Fog huddled all along the docks of the bay.
   - a. You could not see the water because of the fog.
   - b. You are at a football game near a lake.
   - c. You are out in the rain without an umbrella.

4. Gusty winds made a leaf pile hop, skip, and jump.
   - a. The leaves were blowing around.
   - b. The leaves were dancing in the street.
   - c. The leaves were being raked.
5. The cave seemed to yawn as explorers went inside.
   - a. The explorers were very tired.
   - b. The explorers were searching for a place to camp.
   - c. The explorers were going through a large opening.
6. Prickly bushes grabbed at me as I walked through the thick weeds.
   - a. There were prickly bushes that had claws.
   - b. There were thorns on the bushes that scratched me.
   - c. There were evil people hiding in the weeds.
7. There is not much traffic in that sleepy, little town.
   - a. The town is quiet.
   - b. The townspeople are good sleepers.
   - c. The town has no roads.

Just Round It

Directions: Round the following numbers to the nearest 10.

Instrucciones: Redondea los números al 10 más cercano.

1. 15 = ______________
2. 42 = ______________
3. 82 = ______________
4. 22 = ______________
5. 55 = ______________
6. 19 = ______________
7. 39 = ______________
8. 63 = ______________
9. 35 = ______________
10. 11 = ______________
11. 78 = ______________
12. 41 = ______________

Directions: Round the following numbers to the nearest 100.

Instrucciones: Redondea los números al 100 más cercano.

13. 152 = ______________
14. 310 = ______________
15. 425 = ______________
16. 130 = ______________
17. 450 = ______________
18. 721 = ______________
19. 267 = ______________
20. 683 = ______________
21. 888 = ______________
22. 280 = ______________
23. 790 = ______________
24. 901 = ______________

Directions: Round the following numbers to the nearest 1,000.

Instrucciones: Redondea los números al 1000 más cercano.

25. 3,267 = ______________
26. 5,555 = ______________
27. 7,136 = ______________
28. 4,500 = ______________
29. 2,230 = ______________
30. 8,917 = ______________
31. 1,644 = ______________
32. 7,896 = ______________
33. 6,499 = ______________
34. 7,320 = ______________
35. 6,200 = ______________
36. 7,501 = ______________

Make It Interesting

What to Know A **topic sentence** states the main idea and must capture a reader's interest.

Directions: Read the following list of writing ideas. Choose two. Create a topic sentence for each. An example is done for you.

Instrucciones: Lee la lista siguiente sobre ideas de escritura. Elije dos. Crea una oración temática.

- the best place to go swimming
- the best kind of dessert
- the best amusement park ride
- the hardest subject in school
- an enjoyable board game to play

1. For a refreshing dip on a warm day, nothing beats the cool, clear waters of Lake Superior.
2. ____________________
3. ____________________

Directions: Read the following sentences. Rewrite each in the form named below each sentence. The first one is done for you.

Instrucciones: Lea las siguientes oraciones. Vuelve a escribir cada una en la forma nombrada debajo de cada oración. El primer ejemplo es para ti.

4. I wonder if that is a shark swimming over there.
   Rewrite as a question: Is that a shark swimming over there?
5. You should get out of the water soon.
   Rewrite as a command: ____________________
6. I am relieved to see that it is only a dolphin.
   Rewrite as an exclamation: ____________________

Mixed Patterns

Directions: Complete these number patterns.

Instrucciones: Completa estos patrones numéricos.

1. 3, 19, 16, 3, 19, 16, ______, 19, ______, 3, ______, ______, 3, ______, 16, ______, ______, ______

2. 35, 40, 16, 35, ______, 16, ______, ______, ______, 35, ______, ______, ______, ______, ______

3. 6, 7, 8, 6, ______, ______, ______, 7, ______, 6, ______, ______, ______, 7, ______, ______

4. 9, 19, 29, 39, 9, ______, ______, 39, ______, ______, 29, ______, 9, ______, ______, ______

Directions: Complete these picture patterns.

Instrucciones: Completa estos patrones de imágenes.

5. △, ○, ▭, △, ____, ____, ____, ____, ▭, △, ____, ____, ____, ○, ____, △

6. →, ↑, ←, →, ____, ____, ____, ↑, ____, ____, ____, ←, ____, ____, ←

7. ♡, ♡, ○, □, ♡, ____, ○, ____, ♡, ♡, ____, ____, ____, ____, ○, ____, ♡

8. ▭, ▯, ▭, ▯, ____, ____, ____, ____, ____, ▯, ____, ____, ▭, ____, ____

Directions: Look at each pattern and complete the tables.

Instrucciones: Mira cada uno de los patrones y completa las tablas.

9. 

Number of Triangles	1	2	3	6	8	11
Number of Sides						

10. 

Number of Circles	1	2	3	7	9	11
Number of Dots						

Puppy Tale

Directions: Read the story, then circle the correct answers below.

Instrucciones: Lee el cuento, luego, haz un círculo alrededor de las respuestas correctas que figuran a continuación.

Gretchen had wanted a dog for as long as she could remember, but her parents had always said no. This time was different. A puppy had been hanging around their house for two days. It whimpered and seemed hungry. On the second night, Gretchen fed it some of her hot dog. It hadn't left her side since.

The next morning, Gretchen's parents called the animal shelter and reported the missing puppy. They were told that if no one claimed the puppy in 72 hours, the puppy could be theirs. They didn't seem too worried. They knew the owner would show up.

Two days went by without a call. On the third day, it happened. Everyone froze. Gretchen's father answered the phone. Whew! It wasn't the shelter. Thirty minutes later, the phone rang again. Gretchen gasped for air. It was someone selling soaps. Late in the evening, the phone rang again. This time it was the shelter.

The owner showed up at Gretchen's house the next morning. Gretchen hadn't slept at all that night. She couldn't believe it was over. But the owner asked if the family would be interested in adopting the puppy. Gretchen couldn't believe her ears. This was the last pup in the litter. They had been trying to find an owner. The smiles on her parents' faces made Gretchen realize that she was the proud owner of little Miracle.

1. What is this passage mainly about?
   - a. how a puppy can get lost
   - b. the process an owner takes to find a lost animal
   - c. the different types of dogs
   - d. how Gretchen finally received a dog

2. In the third paragraph, what does the word *gasped* mean?
   - a. quickly took in air
   - b. documented
   - c. measured
   - d. opened

3. What improved Gretchen's chances of finally getting a dog?
   - a. A puppy is hard to house train.
   - b. The puppy liked hot dogs.
   - c. An adorable puppy is hard to sell.
   - d. Her parents realized how much Gretchen wanted a dog.

4. Why did Gretchen name her puppy Miracle?
   - a. It was a miracle the puppy had not died.
   - b. Her parents believe in miracles.
   - c. It was a miracle that Gretchen's parents let her keep the dog.
   - d. She had always wanted to name a dog Miracle.

Bicycle Search

Directions: Lots of bits make up a bike—and they're hidden "wheely well." Find the following words in the word search below.

Instrucciones: Muchas partes componen una bicicleta. Encuentra las siguientes palabras en la búsqueda de palabras.

air	BMX	handlebar	mudguard	pump	sprocket	valve
bell	chain	light	oil	seat	tire	wheel
bicycle	gears	mirror	pedal	spoke	tube	

								S	L	D								
						W	P	L	B	I	R	V						
				G	H	R	E	E		R	H	A	A	S				
			C	E	O	B			P			L	U	L	A			
		Y	E	C					E					G	V	H		
		L	K		A				D				I		D	E		
	K	E	C			I			A			M			X	U	S	
	T	O					R		L		R					M	M	
D	T	F						U	U	A						L	B	B
E	H		N	I	A	H	C		B		T	I	R	E	R		C	T
B	G	S						E	P	E						Q	A	E
	I	P					L		U		O					E	L	
	L	O	C			D			M			R			S	C	S	
		K	N		N				P				H		Y	R		
		E	T	A					V					C	A	O		
			H	O	I	L			S			Q	I	E	B			
				E	B	U	T	Q		W	J	B	G	S				
						M	I	R	R	O	R	X						
								H	V	T								

Code Words

The two grids shown here contain the code you will be using to figure out words and to make your own code words.

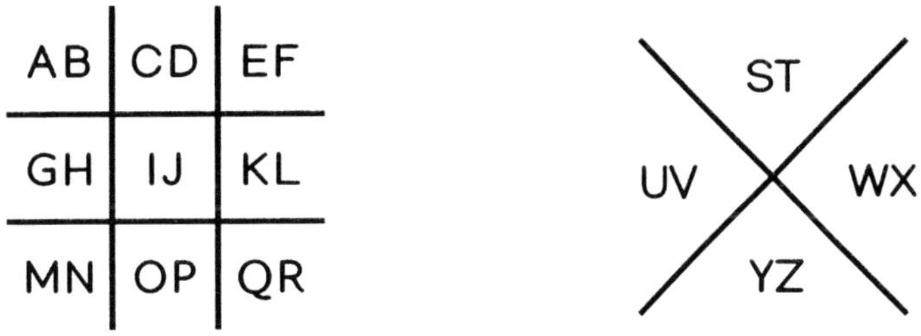

Each letter is represented by the lines that surround it. If it's meant to be the second letter in the box, a dot is used.

Examples:

An **A** looks like this: A **B** looks like this: An **S** looks like this: A **T** looks like this:

Directions: Solve each code. Write the word.

Instrucciones: Resuelve cada código. Escribe la palabra.

1. 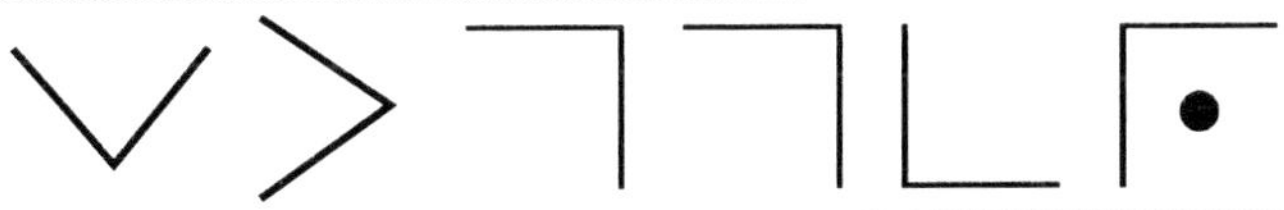 ____________

2.  ____________

3. 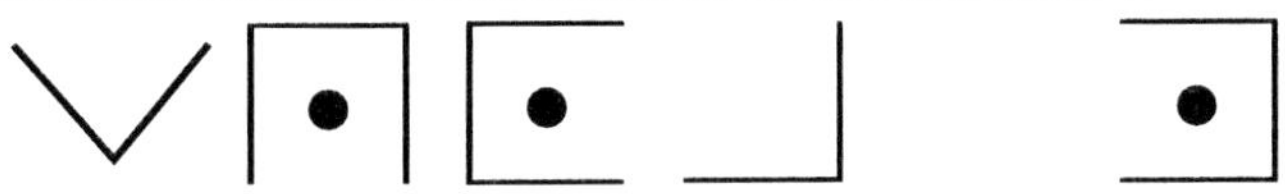 ____________

4.  ____________

5.  ____________

Now it's your turn:

6. Use the code to write your name.

7. Choose any word with 4 or more letters. Write the code here. See if your family members can figure it out.

So Many Variables

Directions: Which equation could help you solve each problem? Write the letter of the correct equation in front of the problem, then solve the equation on the line. Not all of the equations will be used.

Instrucciones: ¿Qué ecuación podría ayudarte a resolver cada problema? Escribe la letra de la ecuación correcta frente al problema, luego resuelve la ecuación en la línea. No todas las ecuaciones serán utilizadas.

a. $21 \div 3 = x$	c. $31 + 14 = b$	e. $12 - p = 4$	g. $21 \times 3 = c$
b. $11 - 4 = p$	d. $100 + v = 113$	f. $25 + s = 42$	h. $8 \times 7 = b$

_____ 1. Karl had 25 stamps. His uncle sent him more. Karl now has 42 stamps.

How many stamps did Karl's uncle send him? _____________________

_____ 2. Debbie packed 8 books in each box. She packed 7 boxes.

How many books did she pack? _____________________

_____ 3. Mike's mom made 21 sandwiches for the picnic. She put 3 in each sack.

How many sacks did she use? _____________________

_____ 4. Ed's dog had 12 puppies. Ed gave some away to friends. Now, he has 4 puppies.

How many puppies did he give away? _____________________

_____ 5. Elisa had 100 songs. Then, she bought some more. Now, she has 113 songs.

How many songs did Elisa buy? _____________________

Directions: Find the value of each expression.

Instrucciones: Encuentra el valor de cada expresión.

6. If r equals 4, what is the value of $r + 6$? _____________________
7. What is the value of $36 \div s$ if s equals 9? _____________________
8. What is the value of $t - 15$ if t equals 21? _____________________
9. If m equals 33, what is the value of $68 - m$? _____________________
10. What is the value of $b + 42$ if b equals 27? _____________________

Lesson Learned

Directions: Read the selection, then answer the questions.

Instrucciones: Lee la selección, luego responde las preguntas.

Once there was a mother mouse who was very proud of her five mouse children. The mouse family lived in the house of a human family. The mouse family worked hard to keep the human home clean. After each meal, the mice would scurry out to pick up crumbs and other things that had dropped to the floor.

It was a busy and hectic life, but this was a hardworking mouse family. That is, except for one family member. Mina Mouse was content to spend her days lying around. She had no desire to work and managed to get out of most of the chores.

One day, Mother Mouse knew that things had to change! She sat Mina down and explained that she had to start carrying her own weight.

"But Mother," protested Mina.

"No, my child. You will one day see the wisdom in this," replied Mother Mouse.

And that day was soon to come. The next morning, Mother gave out assignments. The mice children hurried to get their jobs done so that they could play—that is, except for Mina. She spent her morning complaining.

Suddenly, there was a knock at the door. Mother answered the door and found her neighbor inviting the children to go with them to the circus. Mother allowed all her children to go as long as their chores were done. Everyone had their chores done . . . except for Mina. From that day forward, Mina always managed to get her jobs done first.

1. What did Mother Mouse mean when she talked to Mina about "carrying her own weight"?

____

____

2. What is the meaning of the word *hectic* as used in the second paragraph?

   a. chilly b. frantic c. disruptive d. calm

3. What is the moral of this story?

   a. A bird in the hand is worth two in the bush.

   b. A friend in need is a friend indeed.

   c. Work before play.

What's the Time?

Directions: Write the times from the list below on the digital clocks. Then, draw the hands showing the times on the analog clocks. The first one has been done for you.

Instrucciones: Escribe las horas de la lista de abajo en los relojes digitales. Luego, dibuja las manecillas, mostrando las horas en los relojes analógicos. El primer ejemplo es para ti.

1. twelve minutes past seven
2. six forty-four
3. ten twenty-five
4. six minutes before five
5. twenty-three minutes before three
6. eleven seventeen
7. two thirty-three
8. eighteen minutes after eight

Adjective Attention

What to Know

An **adjective** describes a noun or pronoun. Adjectives usually answer the question *what kind* or *how many.*

Directions: Decide if the adjectives answer the question *what kind* or *how many.* Write your answer on the line. The first two are done for you.

Instrucciones: Decide si los adjetivos responden a la pregunta, qué tipo o cuántos. Escribe tu respuesta en la línea. Los dos primeros ejemplos son para ti.

1. all ____how many____
2. best ____what kind____
3. few ________
4. new ________
5. warm ________
6. blue ________
7. fast ________
8. long ________
9. seven ________
10. white ________
11. a lot ________
12. eight ________
13. funny ________
14. million ________

Directions: Tell if the underlined adjectives answer the question *what kind* or *how many.*

Instrucciones: Indica si los adjetivos subrayados responden a la pregunta *qué tipo* o *cuántos.*

15. There were <u>six</u> birds in our tree. ________
16. <u>Small</u> sparrows are good singers. ________
17. Blue jays eat <u>lots</u> of acorns and nuts. ________
18. An <u>old</u> crow sat on a dead branch. ________

Directions: Circle all the adjectives that answer the question *what kind* or *how many.*

Instrucciones: Encierra en un círculo todos los adjetivos que respondan a la pregunta *qué tipo* o *cuántos.*

19. People, young and old, enjoy watching birds.
20. The only equipment you need is a pair of eyes.
21. Good ears and a guide book are helpful, too.
22. Many bird watchers use powerful binoculars.

Shapes and Angles

Words to Know

Polygon—a closed, two-dimensional figure with three or more straight lines

Quadrilateral—a polygon with four sides and four corners

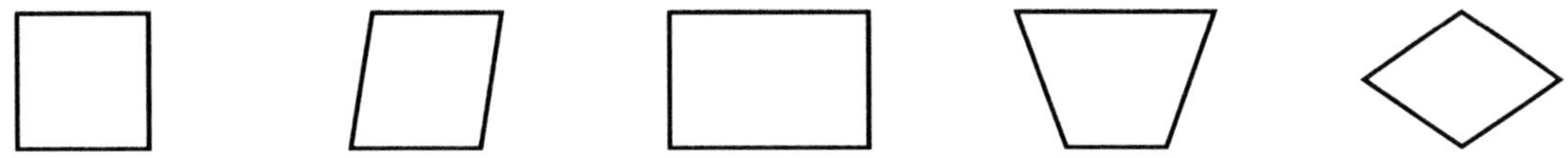

Right angle—an angle that forms a square corner; a 90° angle

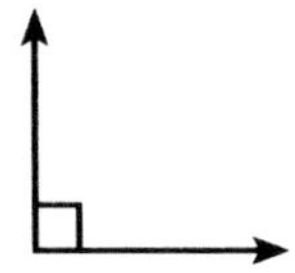

Directions: Color in all of the quadrilaterals.

Instrucciones: Colorea todos los cuadriláteros.

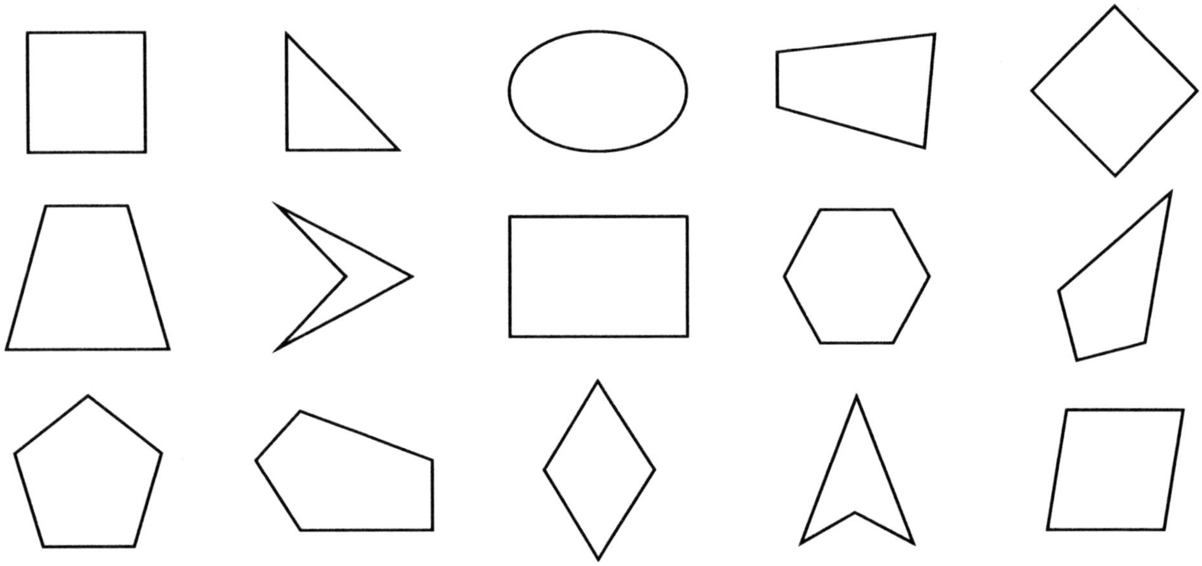

Directions: Draw squares on all of the right angles. The first one has been done for you.

Instrucciones: Dibuja cuadrados en todos los ángulos rectos. El primer ejemplo es para ti.

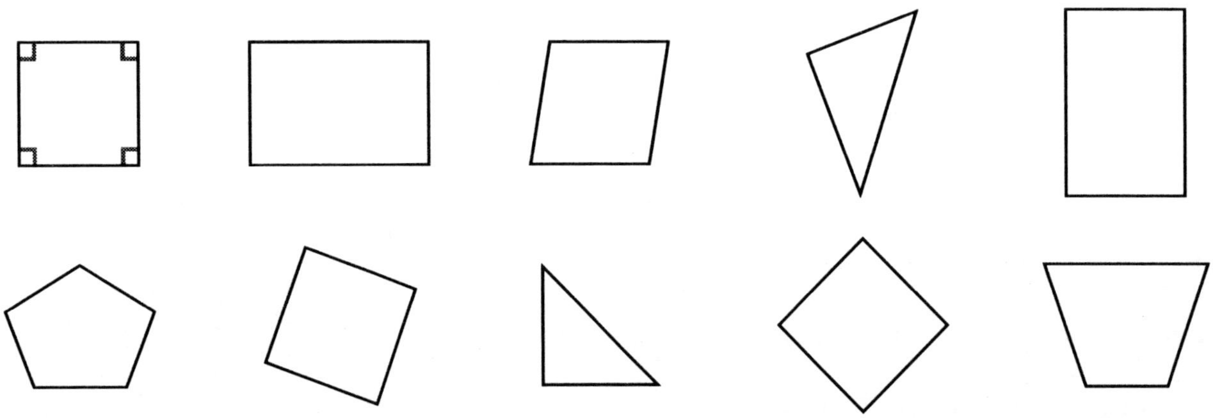

Limericks

What to Know

Limericks are poems that are usually funny and have a regular rhythm (beat) and a regular pattern of rhyming words. Limericks are a popular kind of humorous verse.

Directions: Read the limericks, then complete the activities.

Instrucciones: Lea las quintillas y luego completa las actividades.

Five lines

1.

There once was a boy with a pain
Who said it's a pity again.
Whenever I'm sick
It's surely a trick
There's either no school or no rain.

2.

There was a farmer from **Leeds**
Who ate a packet of **seeds.**
It soon came to pass
He was covered in grass
And couldn't sit down for the **weeds.**

—Sumhika Rao

Rhymes in lines 1, 2, and 5

A common introduction

Rhymes in lines 3 and 4

3.

There was an old man with a beard,
Who said, "It's just as I feared!
Two owls and a **hen,**
Four larks and a **wren,**
Have all built their nests in my beard!"

4.

A mouse in her room woke Miss Dowd
She was frightened, it must be **allowed,**
Soon a happy thought hit her
So to scare off the critter
She sat up in bed and meowed.

Means "agreed"

1. Circle the correct answer. The sick boy feels . . .

   a. cheated. b. that life is unfair. c. both a and b

2. Explain how you think the man from Leeds ended up unable to sit down because of "the weeds."

   ____

   ____

3. Write one sentence explaining why Miss Dowd meowed.

   ____

4. Write an equation to show how many birds are in the man's beard.

   ____

Read the Graphs

Directions: This line graph shows the cost of grapes. Use it to answer the questions.

Instrucciones: Este gráfico lineal muestra el costo de las uvas. Úsalo para responder las preguntas.

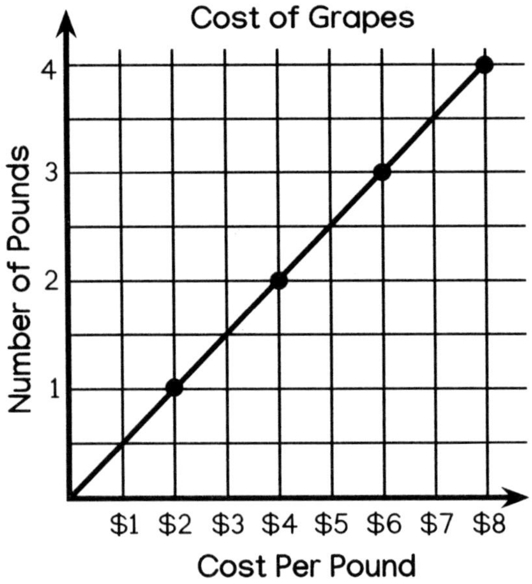

1. How much will 1 pound of grapes cost?

____

2. How much will 3 pounds of grapes cost?

____

3. How many pounds of grapes could you buy for $7?

____

4. How many pounds of grapes could you buy for $1?

____

5. If you spent $5, what would your grapes weigh?

____

6. How much will it cost to buy $1\frac{1}{2}$ pounds of grapes?

____

Directions: This line graph shows the number of books sold over one week. Use it to answer the questions.

Instrucciones: Este gráfico de líneas muestra el número de libros vendidos durante una semana. Úsalo para responder las preguntas.

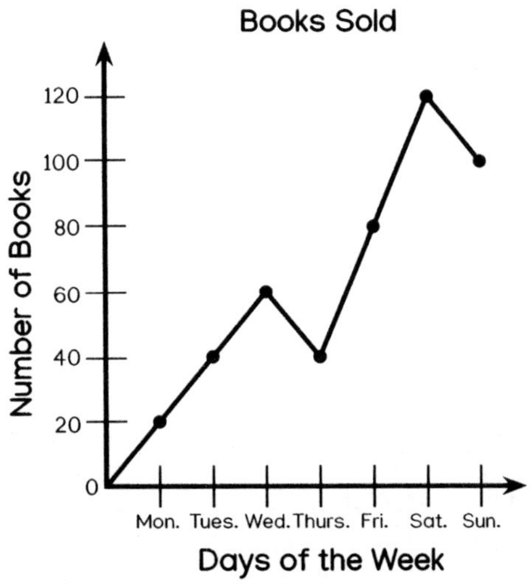

7. What are the two busiest days at the bookshop?

____

8. On which day were the least number of books sold?

____

9. On which day did the shop sell 100 books?

____

10. How many books did the shop sell altogether?

____

What's the Order?

Directions: Put each group into its proper sequence. The first ones are done for you.

Instrucciones: Coloca cada grupo en el orden adecuado. Los primeros ejemplos son para ti.

	Morning Routine
eat	1. wake
wake	2.
dress	3.
leave	4.
brush teeth	5.

	How Jenny Got Stuck in a Tree
Jenny climbed higher.	6. The dog chased Jenny's cat.
The cat climber higher.	7.
The cat raced up the tree.	8.
The dog chased Jenny's cat.	9.
The cat wouldn't come down.	10.
Jenny climbed the tree.	11.
Both were too frightened to climb down.	12.

Directions: Choose two of the following topics, then write a sequence of events for each.

Instrucciones: Elije dos de los siguientes temas, luego escribe una secuencia de los acontecimientos de cada uno.

- When I fell in the river
- When the balloon popped
- When I spilled the milk

13. ______________________________

____

____

____

14. ______________________________

____

____

____

Reverse Words

Directions: Reverse words are words that become different words when read backwards. Write the words and their reverses from the clues below.

Instrucciones: Las palabras inversas son palabras que se convierten en palabras diferentes cuando se leen al revés. Escribe las palabras y sus reversos a partir de las claves de abajo.

Example: physician/fish = doc/cod

1. sticky substance/rodent ____________________
2. not cooked/battle ____________________
3. cooking container/the best ____________________
4. cat and dog/part of staircase ____________________
5. not die/cruel ____________________
6. not later/opposite of lost (as in a race) ____________________
7. half of twenty/tennis court separation ____________________
8. pieces/a belt ____________________
9. flying mammals/knife injury ____________________
10. part of a dresser/prize ____________________

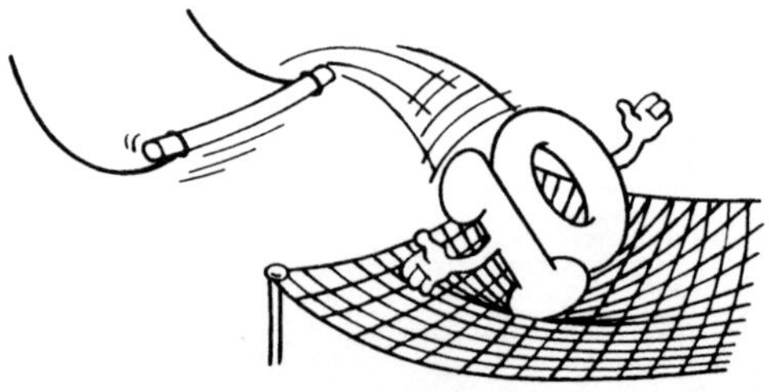

What Comes Next?

Directions: Draw the next shape in each series.

Instrucciones: Dibuja la siguiente forma en cada una de las series.

1.	○ □ □ ○ □ □ ○ □	
2.	♡ △ △ ♡ △ △ ♡ △	
3.	○ ☆ ○ ☆ ○ ☆ ○ ☆	
4.	□ □ □ ◗ ◗ ◗ ♡ ♡	
5.	○ △ ○ ▽ ○ △ ○ ▽	
6.	≡ ☆ □ ≡ ☆ □ ≡ ☆	
7.	□ △ △ ♡ ♡ ♡ ◗ ◗ ◗	
8.	△ △ ○ ○ △ △ □ □ △	
9.	♡ ♡ ☆ ♡ ♡ □ ♡ ♡ ☆ ♡	
10.	□ ↑ □ → □ ↓ □ ← □	

Graphing Favorites

Directions: Study the pie graph, then answer the questions.

Instrucciones: Estudia el gráfico circular y luego responde las preguntas.

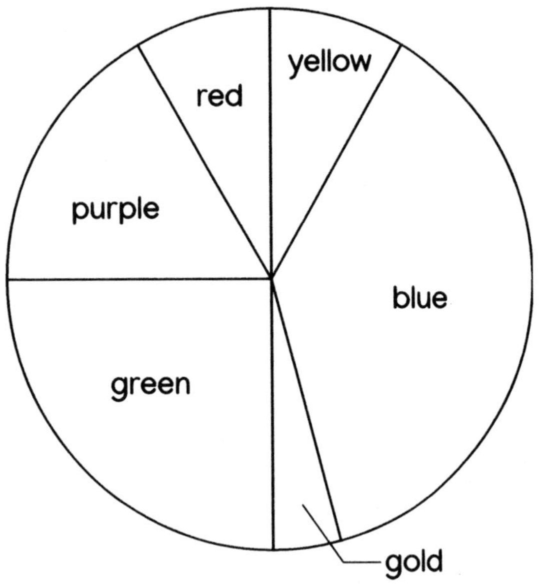

1. What was the most popular color?

   ____

2. What was the least popular color?

   ____

3. Which two colors had the same popularity?

   ____

4. Which color had twice the popularity of red?

   ____

5. Name three colors which make up half the graph.

   ____

Directions: Study the pie graph, then answer the questions.

Instrucciones: Estudia el gráfico circular y luego responde las preguntas.

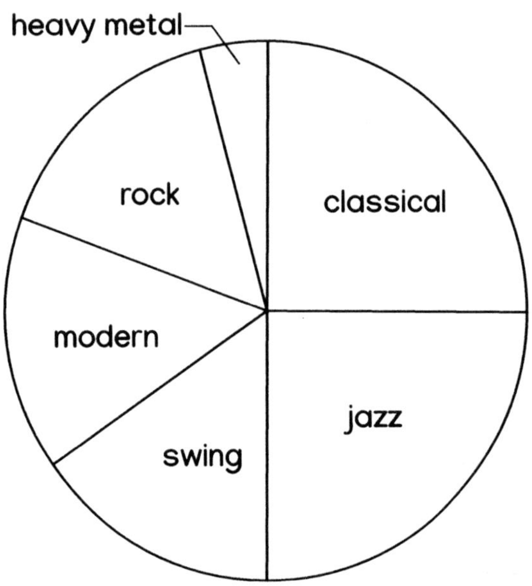

6. Which were the two most popular types of music?

   ____

7. Which was the least popular type of music?

   ____

8. What fraction of the total music selection was jazz?

   ____

9. Which two types of music make up half the total?

   ____

10. What is your favorite type of music?

    ____

Put Them Together

Directions: For each group of sentences below, write one sentence that includes all the necessary information. Use adjectives and adverbs to add description and strengthen the sentence even more. The first one has been done for you.

Instrucciones: Para cada grupo de oraciones a continuación, escribe una oración que incluya todas la información necesaria. Usa adjetivos y adverbios para agregar descripción y fortalecer la oración aún más. El primer ejemplo es para ti.

1. Grandpa read the newspaper.
   Grandpa drank his coffee.
   Grandpa read the Sunday newspaper while he drank his hot coffee.

2. The students played at recess.
   The teachers watched them play.

3. The girl likes picnics.
   The girl likes exploring.

4. The children visited the museum.
   It was a class field trip.

5. The kittens were playful.
   The kittens chased balls.
   The balls had bells on them.

6. Caroline chose a nice spot.
   It was near a brook.
   It was peaceful.

7. A crane came to the building.
   The crane had a wrecking ball.
   The crane knocked down the building.
   People watched it crumble.

Dollars and Cents

Directions: Read each problem below. Write the coins and bills used to count back the change under the problem. The first one has been done for you.

Instrucciones: Lee cada problema a continuación. Escribe las monedas y los billetes utilizados para contar el cambio bajo el problema. El primer ejemplo es para ti.

1. The comic book cost \$5.86. Tim gave the cashier \$10.00. How much change did he receive?

$$\begin{array}{r} 4 \times \$1.00 \\ 1 \times \$\ \ .10 \\ +4 \times \$\ \ .01 \\ \hline \$4.14 \end{array}$$

2. The bill for the Johnson family to get into the movies was \$42.27. Mr. Johnson gave the cashier \$50.00. How much change did he receive?

3. The total cost for the party supplies was \$32.18. Aunt Jenny gave the cashier \$35.00. How much change did she receive?

Directions: Rewrite each problem vertically and solve. Watch your signs.

Instrucciones: Vuelve a escribir cada problema en vertical y resuélvelo. Observa tus signos.

4. \$14.88 – \$9.20	**5.** \$490.01 + \$24.51	**6.** \$159.20 + \$3.10	**7.** \$84.39 – \$62.94

Amphibians

Directions: Read the selection, then circle the letter beside the correct answer.

Instrucciones: Lee la selección, luego haz un círculo alrededor de la letra al costado de la respuesta correcta.

What is an amphibian? An amphibian is an animal that spends part of its life underwater and part on land. When amphibians are underwater, they breathe with gills. When they are on land, they breathe with lungs. They are cold-blooded. This means that their body temperature changes depending on the temperature around them.

There are three different kinds of amphibians. The first group is newts and salamanders. These animals are about three inches long. They have four legs and four **"fingers"** on each leg. They are red-orange and transform to the color green.

The second type is frogs and toads. Frogs and toads are very similar. Toads have a warty back and spend less time in the water. They both eat insects and other small animals. Frogs begin as tadpoles. They spend time close to the water so that they can lay their eggs.

The last group is caecilians. These are wormlike creatures. Millions of years ago, there were other types of amphibians, but they are now extinct.

1. How is an amphibian different than most mammals?
   - a. An amphibian eats different foods.
   - b. An amphibian breathes underwater with gills.
   - c. The amphibian is very territorial.
   - d. An amphibian can swim.

2. Why is the word *fingers* in quotation marks in the passage?
   - a. The author isn't sure it is the right word to use.
   - b. The author is using it to show that they look and work like fingers.
   - c. They don't become fingers until later.
   - d. The author isn't sure of what to call these things.

3. What are the similarities between a frog and a toad?
   - a. They both eat insects and other small animals.
   - b. They are both endangered species.
   - c. They are both wormlike creatures.
   - d. They both begin as tadpoles.

4. What does the passage say about some amphibians millions of years ago?
   - a. There is not enough information about them.
   - b. There are new species being discovered every day.
   - c. They are now extinct.

Time Change

Directions: Read each situation below and write your answers on the lines.

Instrucciones: Lee cada situación que figura a continuación y escribe tus respuestas en las líneas.

1. Grandma is coming in exactly 2 days. In how many hours will Grandma be coming?

   ________________ hours

2. Tom finished the race in 420 seconds. In how many minutes did he finish the race?

   ________________ minutes

3. How many hours are there in 360 minutes?

   ________________ hours

4. How many minutes are there in 2 hours and 18 minutes?

   ________________ minutes

5. How many days are there in 96 hours?

   ________________ days

6. How many seconds are there in 2 minutes and 45 seconds?

   ________________ seconds

7. The movie marathon lasted for 72 hours. How many days did the marathon last?

   ________________ days

8. How many days are there in 5 weeks?

   ________________ days

Describe It

Directions: Adjectives are the describing words that add important details to the nouns in your writing. Underline all of the nouns in the following sentences. Revise the sentences to include one strong adjective before each noun. The first one is done for you.

Instrucciones: Los adjetivos son las palabras descriptivas que agregan detalles importantes a los sustantivos en tu escritura. Subraya todos los sustantivos en las siguientes oraciones. Revisa las oraciones para incluir un adjetivo fuerte antes de cada sustantivo. El ejemplo es para ti.

1. Frightened by the noise, the children cried. Frightened by the loud noise, the scared children cried.
2. The frog hid under a mushroom. ______
3. Dribbling down his chin was sauce. ______
4. A balloon floated into the sky. ______
5. The truck rumbled onto the road. ______
6. Fruit ripened in the basket. ______
7. The quarterback threw a pass to his teammate. ______
8. The sun and wind dried the clothes. ______
9. The boys and girls laughed at the magician. ______
10. In the office, a nurse tended to the child. ______

Math Mix

Directions: Solve the problems. Remember to calculate the parentheses first.

Instrucciones: Resuelve el problema. Recuerda calcular los paréntesis primero.

1. 7 + (3 × 4) = ________	**2.** (6 × 5) + 7 = ________	**3.** (6 × 9) − 3 = ________
4. (8 × 2) + (3 × 4) = ________	**5.** (2 × 10) + (3 × 10) = ________	**6.** (5 × 2) + (6 × 2) = ________
7. (9 × 9) + 9 = ________	**8.** (8 × 3) + 5 = ________	**9.** (7 × 3) + 10 = ________
10. 10 + (3 × 3) = ________	**11.** (3 × 3) + 3 = ________	**12.** (6 × 7) + (6 × 7) = ________

Directions: Find the missing factors.

Instrucciones: Encuentra los factores faltantes.

13. 6 × ________ = 60	**14.** 7 × ________ = 49	**15.** ________ × 8 = 64
16. 10 × ________ = 70	**17.** 5 × ________ = 25	**18.** 9 × ________ = 81
19. 4 × ________ = 24	**20.** 7 × ________ = 14	**21.** 10 × ________ = 0

Directions: Fill in the spaces to complete the patterns.

Instrucciones: Rellena los espacios para completar los patrones.

22. 2, 4, 6, 8, ________, 12	**23.** 6, 9, ________, 15, 18, ________
24. 20, ________, 40, 50, ________, 70	**25.** 21, 28, ________, ________, 49, 56
26. 20, 25, ________, ________, ________	**27.** 16, 24, ________, 40, ________, ________

Pros and Cons

What to Know **Pros and cons** are points for and against an idea that is being discussed. They are usually written in single sentences in order of importance.

Directions: Read the selection, then answer the questions.

Instrucciones: Lee la selección, luego responde las preguntas.

Should Children Always Wear Sunscreen?

The topic is usually a question to be answered.

Pros (For)

Positive points are in order of importance.

1. Children should wear sunscreen all the time because, without it, they can get skin cancer when they are older.
2. If children wear sunscreen continually, they won't get sunburned because sunscreen protects their skin.
3. Exposure to sunlight can cause your skin to age and wrinkle more quickly. Sunscreen prevents this.

One point per number.

Cons (Against)

Reasons make an argument believable.

Negative points are in order of importance.

1. There's no point in wearing sunscreen when we're indoors or when it is raining.
2. People already wear clothes and hats to protect them from the sun, so they don't need to wear sunscreen, too.
3. Some people actually like to have suntanned skin, and sunscreen slows the tanning of their skin.

1. Circle the correct answer. This discussion is about

   a. skin color. b. sunburn. c. wearing sunscreen.

2. Complete this sentence: The most serious effect of going without sunscreen protection

   is ______________________________

3. Do you know what sunburn is? If not, then look it up. Explain in one complete sentence.

   ____

4. Circle the correct answer. Hats protects us against sunburn by

   a. keeping our heads cool.

   b. keeping the sun's rays from our face and ears.

   c. keeping rain off our hair.

Toothpick Test

Directions: Use 12 "toothpicks" and follow the directions. Each box is a continuation of the previous box. Draw the diagrams you complete.

Instrucciones: Use 12 "palillos de dientes" y sigue las instrucciones. Cada caja es una continuación de la caja anterior. Dibuja los diagramas que completes.

1. Start with 12 toothpicks in box 1.
2. In box 2, remove two toothpicks and make 2 squares.
3. In box 3, use your answer from box 2, move two toothpicks and make 3 squares.

1

2

3

The Last Puzzle

Directions: You've made it to the last activity page! Find and circle these 14 ways to say the fun is over. You can find them going down, across, backwards, or diagonally.

Instrucciones: ¡Llegaste a la última página de actividades! Encuentra y haz un círculo alrededor de estas 14 maneras de decir se acabó la diversión. Puedes encontrarlas yendo hacia abajo, transversalmente, hacia atrás o en diagonal.

CLOSED	ENDED	GONE	LATER	SEE YA
COMPLETED	FINAL	GOODBYE	I'M OUT	THAT IS ALL
DONE	FINISHED	LAST	IT'S OVER	

I	A	F	I	N	I	S	H	E	D	C
T	L	L	I	E	Y	B	D	O	O	G
S	G	A	E	N	D	E	D	M	O	O
O	L	D	Y	T	A	H	P	I	N	G
V	S	A	M	E	C	L	O	S	E	D
E	U	S	S	R	E	T	A	L	T	O
R	T	H	A	T	I	S	A	L	L	N
G	O	N	E	C	O	M	E	T	O	E
A	N	D	E	I	M	O	U	T	N	D

What Do You See?

Look at the letters that are **not circled** in the puzzle. Put them in order, and you will spell out a proverb that is hundreds of years old.

☐☐☐ ☐☐☐☐

☐☐☐☐☐☐ ☐☐☐☐

☐☐☐☐ ☐☐ ☐☐ ☐☐☐

Summer Reading List

Uno de los mejores modos de promover el desarrollo educativo durante el verano es mediante la lectura. Afortunadamente, existe una gran variedad de novelas fantásticas y novelas gráficas podrían interesas y cautivar a tu joven lector. Por favor, lee las reseñas y/o lee los libros tú mismo antes de presentárselos a tu hijo, con el fin de determinar si son adecuados para él.

Si lo deseas, puedes utilizar este gráfico (y el que figura en la páginas 93–94) para mantenerte organizado. Utiliza la columna de **Dates** para anotar el día en que tu hijo leyó el libro o cuándo debería devolverlo en la biblioteca. Utiliza la columna de **Notes** como ayuda para recordar lo que has leído en las reseñas de otros lectores o lo que tu hijo pensó del libro tras leerlo.

Dates	Book Information	Notes
	The One and Only Ivan by Katherine Applegate Through the eyes, ears, and thoughts of a warm-hearted gorilla named Ivan, we learn what life is like for a group of animals in a long-failing circus. Then one day, Ivan must find in himself the leader he was born to be in order to fulfill a promise to an old friend. *Themes:* home, family/friendship/community, identity, memory, animal rights	
	The Secret School by Avi Ida Bidson is only 14 years old when she takes over as teacher of a remote one-room schoolhouse after the regular teacher quits. Could Ida be the "secret" teacher of all the students for the rest of the year? *Themes:* following a dream, secrecy, hope	
	El Deafo by Cece Bell This semi-autobiographical graphic novel tells the tale of a girl who becomes ill, loses her hearing, and struggles to adapt and communicate with others. *Themes:* ability/disability, language/communication, family/friendship, acceptance/rejection	
	Keeper of the Doves by Betsy Byars In Kentucky in the late 1880s, five sisters cannot understand why their father takes care of their scary neighbor. *Themes:* family, loyalty, kindness, empathy	
	The Watsons Go to Birmingham—1963 by Christopher Paul Curtis An older brother acts out, which leads to a trip down South for Kenny and the rest of the Watsons. This close Michigan family experiences laughter and frustration on the road toward Alabama and a dark chapter in American history. *Themes:* coming of age, family, race, mortality	
	Because of Winn-Dixie by Kate DiCamillo After losing her mother and moving to a new town, Opal finds just what she needs: a new friend in the form of a loyal and lovable dog. Their lives intersect with a collection of others who have experienced loss, and together they create a community. *Themes:* family/friendship, loss/abandonment, community	

Summer Reading List *(cont.)*

Dates	Book Information	Notes
	Out of My Mind by Sharon M. Draper Melody is extremely intelligent and thoughtful, but no one knows it because her cerebral palsy severely limits her ability to communicate. Then one day she receives a special device that allows her to get her thoughts out of her mind and show who she truly is and has always been. *Themes:* ability/disability, language/communication, family/friendship, acceptance/rejection	
	Boxes for Katje by Candace Fleming In post-war Holland, a Dutch girl receives a care package from an Indiana girl. This act soon becomes a community effort. *Themes:* gratitude, humanity, kindness	
	Escape from Mr. Lemoncello's Library by Chris Grabenstein A contest leads to the opportunity of a lifetime: a chance to be the first to explore (and escape from) a new library designed by the world's greatest game-maker. But can everyone put aside their differences and work together to solve the clues in time to make their escape? *Themes:* teamwork, friendship, identity, creativity	
	The Million Dollar Shot by Dan Gutman Eleven-year-old Eddie lives in a Louisiana trailer park with his widowed mother. A stroke of luck gives him a chance to win a million dollars by sinking a shot at the NBA finals. *Themes:* poverty, life values, future dreams	
	Babymouse #8: Puppy Love by Jennifer L. Holm and Matthew Holm In this graphic novel, Babymouse has had her challenges with pets, but she feels confident that getting a dog will be a different experience. Will Babymouse end up getting the animal of her dreams? *Themes:* love for animals, determination, humor	
	Under the Quilt of Night by Deborah Hopkinson In this beautifully illustrated book, a young slave uses the Underground Railroad to make her escape to the North. *Themes:* courage, hope, friendship	
	Any Small Goodness: A Novel of the Barrio by Tony Johnston Arturo and his family leave Mexico for East Los Angeles in this book that features many short chapters and is an ideal choice for reading aloud. *Themes:* family relationships, cultural differences, coping with difficulties	
	Cleopatra in Space by Mike Maihack In this popular graphic novel, a young Cleopatra is transported in time from early Egypt to a distant future where she must study, train, and fulfill a destiny to save the galaxy from an evil force. *Themes:* coming of age, heroes/villains, destiny, friendship/acceptance	
	A Corner of the Universe by Ann M. Martin Set in the 1960s, this is the story of how a character's world is turned upside down with the arrival of a mentally challenged uncle. *Themes:* difficult family relationships, making the best of a difficult situation	

Summer Reading List *(cont.)*

Dates	Book Information	Notes
	The Girl with 500 Middle Names by Margaret Peterson Haddix Janie realizes that everyone around her has more money than her family, who recently moved to the suburbs so she could go to a better school. *Themes:* life values, pride, family relationships	
	The Hickory Chair by Lisa Rowe Fraustino A blind boy's grandmother dies but leaves him an important gift that impacts his life. *Themes:* multigenerational relationships, grief, passing on of family beliefs	
	Maniac Magee by Jerry Spinelli This Newbery Award book chronicles a resourceful orphan who must make his own way in the world after running away from an impossible living situation. *Themes:* race relationships, making the best of bad situations, hope	
	The Kite Fighters by Linda Sue Park It is 1473 in Korea, and an 11-year-old boy and his older brother must deal with a rivalry when the older boy receives special treatment from his father as they both compete in a New Year kite competition. *Themes:* sibling rivalry, favoritism, family relationships	
	Tadpole by Ruth White Tad needs a home away from his abusive uncle. Even though his cousins are destitute, they welcome him into their home. *Themes:* family love, abusive adults, gratitude	
	Millicent Min, Girl Genius by Lisa Yee An 11-year-old Chinese American girl records the highs and lows of the summer before her senior year in high school. *Themes:* cross-cultural respect, friendship, humor	

Aprovechando al máximo la lectura de verano

Cuando leas estos libros con tu hijo, puedes hacerle las preguntas que aparecen a continuación. El intercambio de preguntas, respuestas e ideas incrementará y potenciará sus habilidades de comprensión lectora. Estimúlalo a explayarse en sus respuestas y explicar sus pensamientos en detalle.

- ¿La portada del libro te provoca deseos de abrirlo y leerlo?
- ¿De qué trata la historia?
- ¿Adónde transcurre la historia? ¿Te gustaría visitar ese sitio?
- ¿Cómo cambian los eventos del cuento a un personaje o lo hacen crecer de alguna manera?
- Nombra un problema del cuento. ¿Cómo reacciona un personaje ante este problema? ¿Está este problema resuelto en el cuento? ¿Si es así, cómo?
- ¿Qué nos enseña o nos muestra el cuento acerca de la vida?
- ¿Recomendarías este libro a tus amigos? ¿Por qué sí o por qué no?

Read and Do

A continuación, se incluyen algunas ideas divertidas para que tu hijo incremente su lectura. La mayoría implicarán la participación de ambos, pero se encuentran dirigidas hacia él con el fin de incentivar su amor por los libros.

Reading Survey __/__/__	Conduct a survey to find out which books the people in your community loved as children. Include coaches, grocery-store cashiers, babysitters, and other adults you know. Share your findings with friends in order to create an even larger list so that you will always have good book recommendations!
Write to the Author __/__/__	Many authors love to hear from their readers, especially when they hear what people liked best about their books. You can write to an author and send your letter in care of the book's publisher. The publisher's address is listed directly after the title page. Or you may go to the author's website and follow the directions for how to send the author a letter. (To make sure your author is still living, type the author's name into an online search engine.)
A Comic Book __/__/__	Turn your favorite book into a comic book. Fold at least two sheets of paper in half, and staple them so they make a book. With a ruler and pencil, draw boxes across each page to look like blank comic strips. Then, draw the story of your book as if it were a comic. Draw pictures of your characters, and have words coming out of their mouths—just as in a real comic strip.
Write a Sequel __/__/__	What happens to the characters in your book after you finish reading the final page? Why not create a sequel? A sequel is a book that is published after the first book has enjoyed success among readers. Sequels generally pick up where the first book left off. For example, the sequel to Madeleine L'Engle's novel *A Wrinkle in Time* is *A Wind in the Door.*
Learn a New Skill __/__/__	What skills are mentioned in your favorite book? Perhaps a character learns to ride a unicycle. Other characters may create beautiful pottery, train dogs, take black-and-white photographs, or bake five-layer cakes. Identify a skill mentioned in your book. Gather together the materials you'll need to learn this skill. Keep in mind that learning a new skill may take several weeks or months. Commit to practicing this skill at least twice a week. Keep a journal detailing your growing abilities.
Photo Glossary __/__/__	Create a "photo" glossary of the book you have read. Draw pictures of some important places and objects from the book. Beside each, tell what it is and why it is important to the plot, characters, or themes of the book.
How I Felt __/__/__	How did this novel make you feel as you read it? Create a page of words, pictures, and colors that you feel describe the mood of the novel.

Read–Together Chart

Does your father read books to you before bed? Perhaps your mother reads to the family at breakfast? Your grandparents may enjoy reading books to you after school or on the weekends. You and your family members can create a Read–Together Chart and fill it in to keep track of all the books you've read together.

Here are two Read–Together Charts. The first one is a sample. The second one has been left blank, so you can add your own categories and books.

Book We Read	Who Read It?	What It's About	Our Review
Holes	My mom and my dad read it to me.	It's about a family curse that is broken by a boy who learns to believe in himself.	Great book! Way to go, Stanley! This book had parts that made me laugh and parts that made me mad when people didn't treat others very nicely.

This page may be reproduced as many times as needed.

Learning Experiences

A continuación, se incluyen algunas actividades divertidas y de bajo costo que puedes realizar junto a tu hijo. Pronto descubrirás que las mismas pueden ser estimulantes, educativas y complementarias del resto de los ejercicios del libro.

Tarjetas didácticas __/__/__	Elabora todo tipo de tarjetas didácticas. Dependiendo de los intereses de tu hijo y su grado académico, pueden incluir letras del abecedario, palabras de uso frecuente, o problemas matemáticos. Puedes crearlas tú mismo con marcadores o en una computadora. Sugiérele que te ayude a cortar imágenes de revistas y péguenlas en tarjetas de 3" x 5". Luego, busca un sitio al aire libre y repasen las tarjetas juntos.
Proyecto de despensa __/__/__	Encuentra un sitio en tu casa donde puedas almacenar víveres. Puede ser un armario o un contenedor que permanezca siempre en el mismo sitio. Busca algunas latas de pintura limpias o baldes. Llénalos con todo tipo de materiales para hacer manualidades. Además de las clásicas pinturas, marcadores, papel, tijeras y pegamento, puedes incluir artículos inusuales, tales como azulejos, flores artificiales y papel de regalo. De este modo, cada vez tú y tu hijo quieran hacer una manualidad, pueden acceder a todo lo necesario en ese preciso momento.
¿Cuanto cuesta? __/__/__	Si salen a comer, pide ayuda a tu hijo para obtener el total de la cuenta. Anoten el costo de la comida de cada comensal. Luego, dile que lo sume y calcule cuánto se gastó en total. Puedes modificar la actividad y volverla mucho más simple, pidiéndole que sólo calcule el costo de una entrada y un trago del menú, o el costo de tres postres. Asegúrate de redondear las cifras primero.
Búsqueda del tesoro en la naturaleza __/__/__	Salgan a caminar, vayan a un parque o realicen una excursión a las montañas. Pero antes de partir, elabora una búsqueda del tesoro para tu hijo. Puede incluir todo tipo de cosas que se puedan encontrar en la naturaleza. Asegúrate que cuente con una bolsa para guardar todo lo que encuentre (y recuerda verificar con anticipación las reglas o leyes relacionadas con la sustracción de cualquier objeto). Puedes incluir cosas tales como: una hoja con bordes puntiagudos, una roca moteada, y una ramita con dos pequeñas ramificaciones. Tómense unos minutos para observar todos los elementos que ha recolectado y táchenlos de la lista.
Realiza un viaje y lleva un diario __/__/__	Si van a realizar un viaje durante el verano, pídele a tu hijo que lleve un diario. Los niños pequeños pueden recolectar postales y pegarlas en un diario en blanco. También pueden dibujar los sitios que visitaron. Si tiene acceso a una cámara de fotos, puede armar un álbum fotográfico.

Cursive Writing Chart

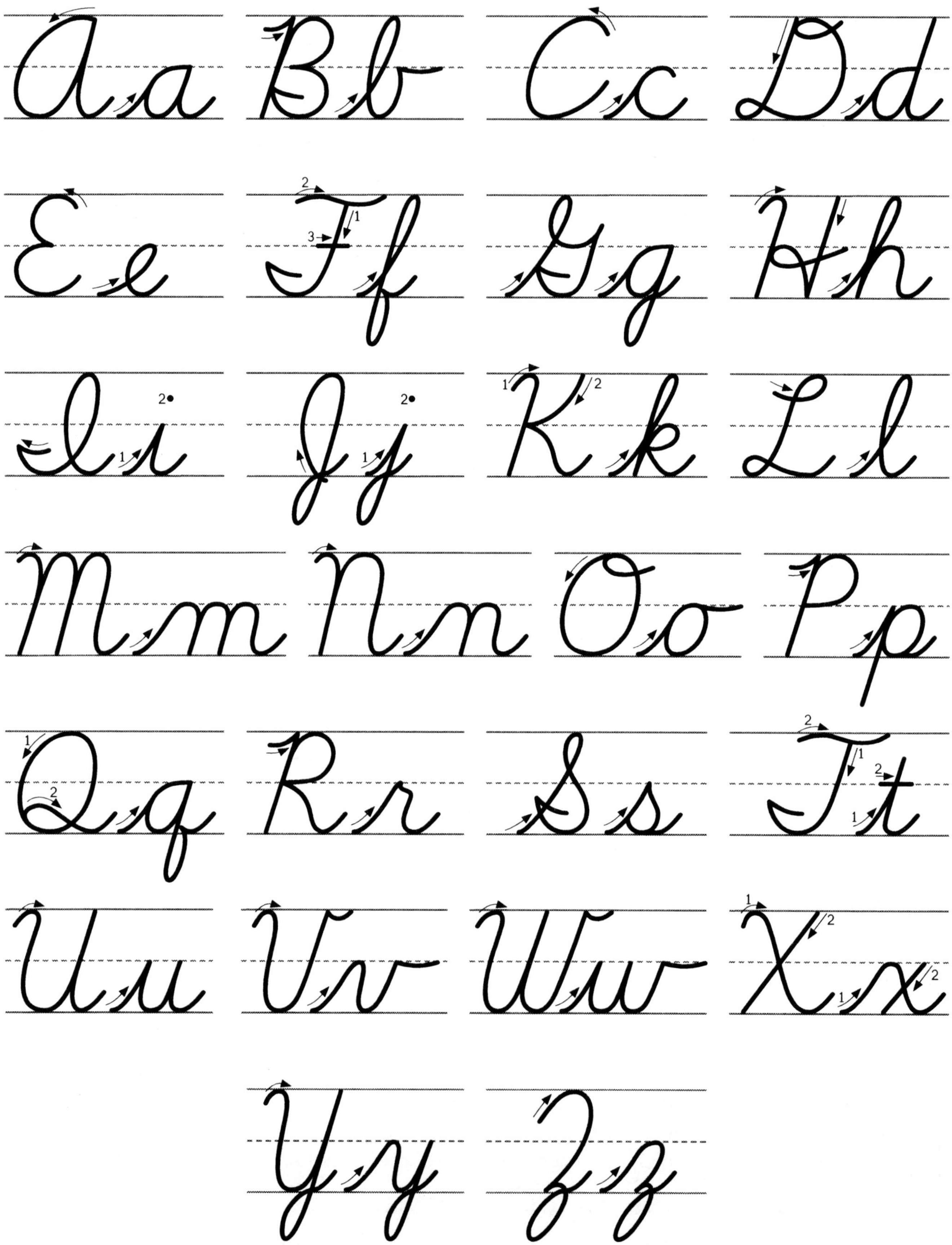

Multiplication Chart

×	0	1	2	3	4	5	6	7	8	9	10	11	12
0	0	0	0	0	0	0	0	0	0	0	0	0	0
1	0	1	2	3	4	5	6	7	8	9	10	11	12
2	0	2	4	6	8	10	12	14	16	18	20	22	24
3	0	3	6	9	12	15	18	21	24	27	30	33	36
4	0	4	8	12	16	20	24	28	32	36	40	44	48
5	0	5	10	15	20	25	30	35	40	45	50	55	60
6	0	6	12	18	24	30	36	42	48	54	60	66	72
7	0	7	14	21	28	35	42	49	56	63	70	77	84
8	0	8	16	24	32	40	48	56	64	72	80	88	96
9	0	9	18	27	36	45	54	63	72	81	90	99	108
10	0	10	20	30	40	50	60	70	80	90	100	110	120
11	0	11	22	33	44	55	66	77	88	99	110	121	132
12	0	12	24	36	48	60	72	84	96	108	120	132	144

Times Tables

1 times table
1 × 0 = 0
1 × 1 = 1
1 × 2 = 2
1 × 3 = 3
1 × 4 = 4
1 × 5 = 5
1 × 6 = 6
1 × 7 = 7
1 × 8 = 8
1 × 9 = 9
1 × 10 = 10
1 × 11 = 11
1 × 12 = 12

2 times table
2 × 0 = 0
2 × 1 = 2
2 × 2 = 4
2 × 3 = 6
2 × 4 = 8
2 × 5 = 10
2 × 6 = 12
2 × 7 = 14
2 × 8 = 16
2 × 9 = 18
2 × 10 = 20
2 × 11 = 22
2 × 12 = 24

3 times table
3 × 0 = 0
3 × 1 = 3
3 × 2 = 6
3 × 3 = 9
3 × 4 = 12
3 × 5 = 15
3 × 6 = 18
3 × 7 = 21
3 × 8 = 24
3 × 9 = 27
3 × 10 = 30
3 × 11 = 33
3 × 12 = 36

4 times table
4 × 0 = 0
4 × 1 = 4
4 × 2 = 8
4 × 3 = 12
4 × 4 = 16
4 × 5 = 20
4 × 6 = 24
4 × 7 = 28
4 × 8 = 32
4 × 9 = 36
4 × 10 = 40
4 × 11 = 44
4 × 12 = 48

5 times table
5 × 0 = 0
5 × 1 = 5
5 × 2 = 10
5 × 3 = 15
5 × 4 = 20
5 × 5 = 25
5 × 6 = 30
5 × 7 = 35
5 × 8 = 40
5 × 9 = 45
5 × 10 = 50
5 × 11 = 55
5 × 12 = 60

6 times table
6 × 0 = 0
6 × 1 = 6
6 × 2 = 12
6 × 3 = 18
6 × 4 = 24
6 × 5 = 30
6 × 6 = 36
6 × 7 = 42
6 × 8 = 48
6 × 9 = 54
6 × 10 = 60
6 × 11 = 66
6 × 12 = 72

Times Tables *(cont.)*

7 times table
7 × 0 = 0
7 × 1 = 7
7 × 2 = 14
7 × 3 = 21
7 × 4 = 28
7 × 5 = 35
7 × 6 = 42
7 × 7 = 49
7 × 8 = 56
7 × 9 = 63
7 × 10 = 70
7 × 11 = 77
7 × 12 = 84

8 times table
8 × 0 = 0
8 × 1 = 8
8 × 2 = 16
8 × 3 = 24
8 × 4 = 32
8 × 5 = 40
8 × 6 = 48
8 × 7 = 56
8 × 8 = 64
8 × 9 = 72
8 × 10 = 80
8 × 11 = 88
8 × 12 = 96

9 times table
9 × 0 = 0
9 × 1 = 9
9 × 2 = 18
9 × 3 = 27
9 × 4 = 36
9 × 5 = 45
9 × 6 = 54
9 × 7 = 63
9 × 8 = 72
9 × 9 = 81
9 × 10 = 90
9 × 11 = 99
9 × 12 = 108

10 times table
10 × 0 = 0
10 × 1 = 10
10 × 2 = 20
10 × 3 = 30
10 × 4 = 40
10 × 5 = 50
10 × 6 = 60
10 × 7 = 70
10 × 8 = 80
10 × 9 = 90
10 × 10 = 100
10 × 11 = 110
10 × 12 = 120

11 times table
11 × 0 = 0
11 × 1 = 11
11 × 2 = 22
11 × 3 = 33
11 × 4 = 44
11 × 5 = 55
11 × 6 = 66
11 × 7 = 77
11 × 8 = 88
11 × 9 = 99
11 × 10 = 110
11 × 11 = 121
11 × 12 = 132

12 times table
12 × 0 = 0
12 × 1 = 12
12 × 2 = 24
12 × 3 = 36
12 × 4 = 48
12 × 5 = 60
12 × 6 = 72
12 × 7 = 84
12 × 8 = 96
12 × 9 = 108
12 × 10 = 120
12 × 11 = 132
12 × 12 = 144

Division Tables

Divided by 1
1 ÷ 1 = 1
2 ÷ 1 = 2
3 ÷ 1 = 3
4 ÷ 1 = 4
5 ÷ 1 = 5
6 ÷ 1 = 6
7 ÷ 1 = 7
8 ÷ 1 = 8
9 ÷ 1 = 9
10 ÷ 1 = 10
11 ÷ 1 = 11
12 ÷ 1 = 12

Divided by 2
2 ÷ 2 = 1
4 ÷ 2 = 2
6 ÷ 2 = 3
8 ÷ 2 = 4
10 ÷ 2 = 5
12 ÷ 2 = 6
14 ÷ 2 = 7
16 ÷ 2 = 8
18 ÷ 2 = 9
20 ÷ 2 = 10
22 ÷ 2 = 11
24 ÷ 2 = 12

Divided by 3
3 ÷ 3 = 1
6 ÷ 3 = 2
9 ÷ 3 = 3
12 ÷ 3 = 4
15 ÷ 3 = 5
18 ÷ 3 = 6
21 ÷ 3 = 7
24 ÷ 3 = 8
27 ÷ 3 = 9
30 ÷ 3 = 10
33 ÷ 3 = 11
36 ÷ 3 = 12

Divided by 4
4 ÷ 4 = 1
8 ÷ 4 = 2
12 ÷ 4 = 3
16 ÷ 4 = 4
20 ÷ 4 = 5
24 ÷ 4 = 6
28 ÷ 4 = 7
32 ÷ 4 = 8
36 ÷ 4 = 9
40 ÷ 4 = 10
44 ÷ 4 = 11
48 ÷ 4 = 12

Divided by 5
5 ÷ 5 = 1
10 ÷ 5 = 2
15 ÷ 5 = 3
20 ÷ 5 = 4
25 ÷ 5 = 5
30 ÷ 5 = 6
35 ÷ 5 = 7
40 ÷ 5 = 8
45 ÷ 5 = 9
50 ÷ 5 = 10
55 ÷ 5 = 11
60 ÷ 5 = 12

Divided by 6
6 ÷ 6 = 1
12 ÷ 6 = 2
18 ÷ 6 = 3
24 ÷ 6 = 4
30 ÷ 6 = 5
36 ÷ 6 = 6
42 ÷ 6 = 7
48 ÷ 6 = 8
54 ÷ 6 = 9
60 ÷ 6 = 10
66 ÷ 6 = 11
72 ÷ 6 = 12

Division Tables *(cont.)*

Divided by 7
7 ÷ 7 = 1
14 ÷ 7 = 2
21 ÷ 7 = 3
28 ÷ 7 = 4
35 ÷ 7 = 5
42 ÷ 7 = 6
49 ÷ 7 = 7
56 ÷ 7 = 8
63 ÷ 7 = 9
70 ÷ 7 = 10
77 ÷ 7 = 11
84 ÷ 7 = 12

Divided by 8
8 ÷ 8 = 1
16 ÷ 8 = 2
24 ÷ 8 = 3
32 ÷ 8 = 4
40 ÷ 8 = 5
48 ÷ 8 = 6
56 ÷ 8 = 7
64 ÷ 8 = 8
72 ÷ 8 = 9
80 ÷ 8 = 10
88 ÷ 8 = 11
96 ÷ 8 = 12

Divided by 9
9 ÷ 9 = 1
18 ÷ 9 = 2
27 ÷ 9 = 3
36 ÷ 9 = 4
45 ÷ 9 = 5
54 ÷ 9 = 6
63 ÷ 9 = 7
72 ÷ 9 = 8
81 ÷ 9 = 9
90 ÷ 9 = 10
99 ÷ 9 = 11
108 ÷ 9 = 12

Divided by 10
10 ÷ 10 = 1
20 ÷ 10 = 2
30 ÷ 10 = 3
40 ÷ 10 = 4
50 ÷ 10 = 5
60 ÷ 10 = 6
70 ÷ 10 = 7
80 ÷ 10 = 8
90 ÷ 10 = 9
100 ÷ 10 = 10
110 ÷ 10 = 11
120 ÷ 10 = 12

Divided by 11
11 ÷ 11 = 1
22 ÷ 11 = 2
33 ÷ 11 = 3
44 ÷ 11 = 4
55 ÷ 11 = 5
66 ÷ 11 = 6
77 ÷ 11 = 7
88 ÷ 11 = 8
99 ÷ 11 = 9
110 ÷ 11 = 10
121 ÷ 11 = 11
132 ÷ 11 = 12

Divided by 12
12 ÷ 12 = 1
24 ÷ 12 = 2
36 ÷ 12 = 3
48 ÷ 12 = 4
60 ÷ 12 = 5
72 ÷ 12 = 6
84 ÷ 12 = 7
96 ÷ 12 = 8
108 ÷ 12 = 9
120 ÷ 12 = 10
132 ÷ 12 = 11
144 ÷ 12 = 12

Proofreading Marks

Editor's Mark	Meaning	Example
≡	capitalize	they fished in lake tahoe.
/	make it lowercase	Five Students missed the Bus.
sp.	spelling mistake	The day was clowdy and cold. (sp.)
⊙	add a period	Tomorrow is a holiday⊙
	delete (remove)	One person knew the the answer.
∧	add a word	Six∧were in the litter. (pups)
∧,	add a comma	He planted peas∧corn, and squash.
∽	reverse words or letters	An otter swam in the bed kelp.
∨’	add an apostrophe	The child’s bike was blue.
∨“ ∨”	add quotation marks	“Why can’t I go?” she cried.
#	make a space	He ate two redapples. (#)
⁀‿	close the space	Her favorite game is soft ball.
¶	begin a new paragraph	to know. ¶Next on the list

Answer Key

Page 12

1. 15,481 **2.** 226 **3.** 2,785 **4.** 8,494 **5.** 1,495 **6.** 16,218

Page 13

1. e **2.** a **3.** b **4.** c **5.** d **6.** helm **7.** drowsy **8.** conform **9.** essential **10.** surroundings

Page 14

1. 90° **2.** 180° **3.** 360° **4.** 360° **5.** 180° **6.** 270° **7.** 270° **8.** 360° **9.** 180°

Page 16

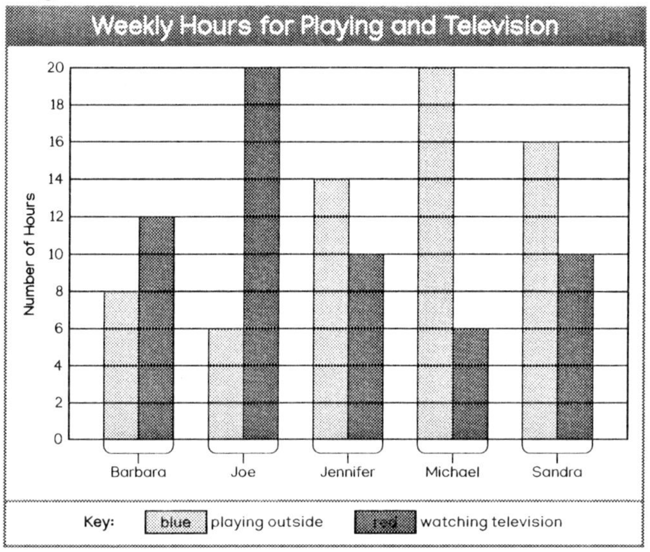

Page 17

Answers will vary; possible answers:

- *Main Idea:* Tiger was a funny cat.
- *Supporting Detail:* He drank from the aquarium.
- *Supporting Detail:* He would lap up the water when they gave the dog a bath.

Page 18

1. $\frac{4}{7}$ **2.** $\frac{1}{6}$ **3.** $\frac{3}{10}$ **4.** $\frac{3}{8}$ **5.** $\frac{1}{3}$

Page 20

1. beach **2.** goggles **3.** swim **4.** float **5.** sand **6.** waves **7.** shells **8.** towel **9.** splash **10.** flippers **11.** lotion **12.** kites

Page 21

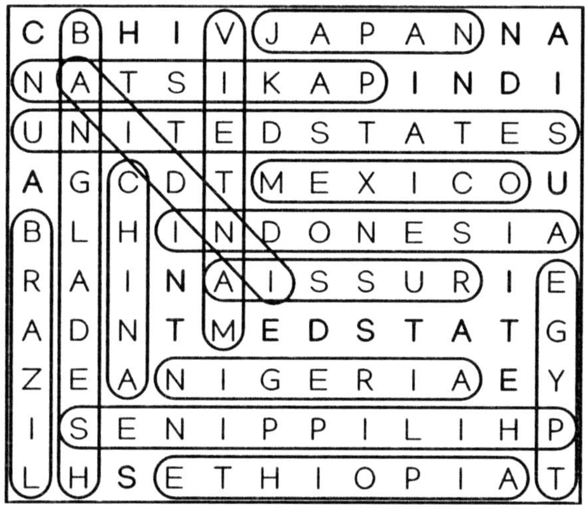

Final Question: 1. China; 2. India; 3. United States

Page 22

1. c **2.** b **3.** 60 stuffed bears **4.** 37 birds

Page 23

1. present **2.** future **3.** past **4.** present **5.** past

6. Maria always **wore** a T-shirt over her bathing suit in the pool.

7. We **pitched** a tent for shade when we **went** on a picnic.

8. The day **was** hot and bright, so we **wore** hats and sunscreen.

Page 24

1. 24 sides **2.** c **3.** 50°F **4.** 28 ft.

Page 25

1. a **2.** b **3.** b

Page 26

Row 1: 6, 12, 6
Row 2: 8, 9, 12
Row 3: 9, 4, 6
Row 4: 9, 7, 5
Row 5: 6, 4, 7
Row 6: 7, 9, 7
Row 7: 6, 9, 4
Row 8: 9, 8, 6

Answer Key *(cont.)*

Page 28

1. \$49 + \$57 = \$106
2. \$32 + \$57 = \$89
3. \$26 + \$32 = \$58
4. \$64 + \$17 + \$49 = \$130
5. \$17 + \$64 = \$81
6. \$26 + \$57 + \$32 = \$115

Page 29

1. 4th **2.** 1st **3.** 3rd **4.** 6th **5.** 2nd **6.** 5th

Page 30

1. 476 **2.** 61 **3.** 810 **4.** 954 **5.** 977

Page 31

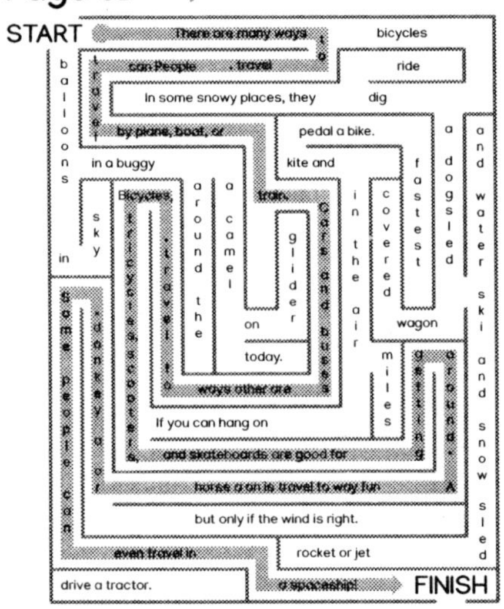

Page 32

1. 100 books
2. mystery
3. 30 more books
4. joke; mystery
5. 50 cones
6. strawberry
7. 20 more cones
8. 180 cones

Page 33

Answers will vary. Possible answers:

1. They are moving to a colder climate.
2. Dishes have been wrapped in newspaper. Larry said, "It might be some time before I see you again." Larry said, "No more beach clothes for you!"

Page 34

2. \$70.34
3. \$5.08
4. \$31.89
5. \$57.14
6. \$6.74
7. \$17.87
8. \$5.09
9. \$5.73
10. \$11.94

Page 35

1. The school
2. The dog
3. The sun
4. Fourth graders
5. Spring

Page 36

1. b
2. 36 candy bars
3. \$1,575
4. 192 cans

Page 37

1. b **2.** b **3.** c

Page 38

1. a **2.** b **3.** b

Page 39

2. Everyone was laughing.
3. Erika has a cold.
4. The cat jumped off the log.
5. They ate the birthday cake.
6. She can do a backward flip.
7. Summer is the time for fishing.

Page 40

Answers will vary. Some possible answers:

1. fin, find, foil, fond, fold, fob, fill
2. left, lent, lend, lam, lit, lid, lad, life, lie, lime, let, lint, leaf, lean, lame, led, lane, late, land, lain, laid, lead, lift, line, lied, lifted, lined, lite
3. call, carts, calls, car, cart, cars, cast, cabs, cab, crab, crabs, cat, cats, crib, cribs

Page 41

Triangles = 27 Quadrilaterals = 40

Page 42

3. 73 R1
4. 132 R3
5. 123 R2
6. 96 R1
7. 72 R5
8. 36 R5
9. 214 R1
10. 45 R3
11. 104 R1
12. 89 R6

Page 44

1. c
2. a. 30, b. 6, c. 15, d. 18, e. 6, f. 3
3. Top to bottom: orange, yellow, green, white

Answer Key *(cont.)*

Page 45

1. about 24 inches
2. July
3. A **1** should be written on the middle fingernail, and a **4** should be written on the pinkie fingernail.

Page 46

1. 90 **2.** 70 **3.** 80 **4.** 24 **5.** 29 **6.** 88

Page 48

1. 40	**5.** 5,300	**9.** 53 things
2. 80	**6.** 900	**10.** 7 years old
3. 60	**7.** 700	
4. 190	**8.** 700	

Page 49

1. a	**3.** b	**5.** d	**7.** A	**9.** S
2. e	**4.** c	**6.** S	**8.** A	**10.** A

Page 50

Anne—volleyball
Elise—basketball
Ethan—swimming
Katie—baseball
Kevin—track
Logan—soccer

Page 51

Answers will vary. Possible answers:

1. The figures in Set A are divided symmetrically in half using a vertical line.
2. The figures in Set B are circular figures. Each shape is rounded on the outer edge.

Page 52

1. d	**4.** b	**7.** b
2. c	**5.** a	**8.** d
3. a	**6.** c	**9.** 600 inches

Page 53

Answers may vary. Possible answers:

2. Yes. Johnny came in at 8:25, exactly 10 minutes after the bell rang.
3. No. His hair and clothes are messy.
4. Yes. He is wearing a heavy coat.
5. No. Mrs. Maddox says, "Again, Johnny?"

Page 54

1–9. All answers are ÷ and =.

10. 42 ÷ 6 = **7**	**15.** 28 ÷ 4 = **7**	**20.** 1 R2
11. 9 ÷ 3 = **3**	**16.** 45 ÷ 5 = **9**	**21.** 3 R1
12. 21 ÷ 7 = **3**	**17.** 6 ÷ 6 = **1**	**22.** 2 R1
13. 36 ÷ 6 = **6**	**18.** 32 ÷ 8 = **4**	**23.** 4 R2
14. 10 ÷ 2 = **5**	**19.** 4 R4	**24.** 2 R1

Page 55

1. **W**hen **I** went to the store, **I** saw my teacher, **M**rs. **R**ose.
2. **M**y family will go to **D**isneyland in **J**uly.
3. **I** am reading Old Yeller this week.
4. **M**y sister **S**arah says her favorite subject is **S**panish.
5. **O**n **W**ednesday, we will celebrate **G**roundhog **D**ay.
6. **M**y brother said that **M**om was a cheerleader at **E**astside **H**igh **S**chool.
7. **I**n **A**ugust, we're going to visit **A**unt **M**ary in **S**an **F**rancisco, **C**alifornia.
8. **B**enji had a birthday, so we sang "**H**appy **B**irthday to **Y**ou."
9. **M**y friend **R**osa speaks **S**panish, and **I** speak **E**nglish.
10. **M**y neighbor **J**ulia is going to **P**aris, **F**rance, next **J**une.

Page 56

Estimates will vary for answers 1–8.

1. 1 hr. 45 min.	**5.** 3 hr. 7 min.
2. 1 hr. 2 min.	**6.** 2 hr. 40 min.
3. 1 hr. 5 min.	**7.** 3 hr. 38 min.
4. 2 hr. 51 min.	**8.** 4 hr. 20 min.

Remaining answers will vary.

Page 57

Answers will vary. Underlined sentences:

1. Today, however, her father was in an especially happy mood and agreed that she could use his car for the afternoon.
2. As Jessica pulled out of the driveway, her favorite song came on, so she turned up the volume on the radio.
3. Jessica swerved to miss the dog and ended up running into the neighbors' trash cans.

Answer Key (cont.)

Page 58

1. 0.6
2. 0.4
3. 0.09
4. 48.07
5. 2.7
6. 9.3
7. $\frac{7}{10}$
8. $\frac{2}{10}$
9. 2 slices
10. $6.25

Page 60

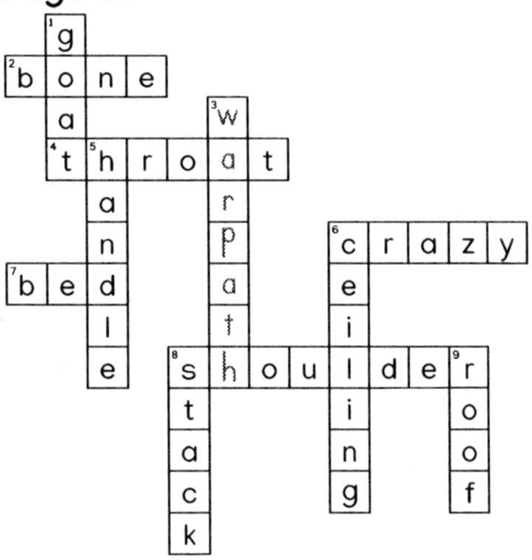

Page 61

1. pay
2. hold
3. move
4. make
5. enjoy
6. bring
7. want
8. keep

Page 62

1. 624 feet
2. 325 feet
3. 358 feet
4. 195 feet
5. 4,875 feet; 405 feet
6. 61.54 meters
7. 6.15 meters
8. 23.08 meters

Page 63

1. Chato and the Party Animals
2. "Years Later"
3. Puppy Dog Pals
4. "Dogs Are Man's Best Friend"
5. Wicked
6. 20,000 Leagues Under the Sea
7. Up
8. The Wizard of Oz
9. "The Road Not Taken"
10. The Indian in the Cupboard

Page 64

1. 500 + 60 + 1
2. 9,000 + 10 + 1
3. 3,000 + 500 + 80 + 7
4. 4,000 + 400 + 4
5. 800 + 20 + 6
6. 8,000 + 900 + 90
8. 590 = five hundreds, eight tens, ten ones
9. 1,028 = (1 × 1,000) + (2 × 10) + (8 × 1)
10. 84 = seven tens, fourteen ones
11. 600 = six one-hundreds
12. 2,300 = no ones, no tens, three hundreds, two thousands
13. 875 = 800 + 70 + 5
14. 9,437 = seven ones, three tens, four hundreds, nine thousands
15. 1,902 = nineteen hundreds, two ones
16. 1,316
17. 4,406
18. 846

Page 65

2. ate away; b
3. huddled; a
4. hop, skip, and jump; a
5. yawn; c
6. grabbed; b
7. sleepy; a

Page 66

1. 20
2. 40
3. 80
4. 20
5. 60
6. 20
7. 40
8. 60
9. 40
10. 10
11. 80
12. 40
13. 200
14. 300
15. 400
16. 100
17. 500
18. 700
19. 300
20. 700
21. 900
22. 300
23. 800
24. 900
25. 3,000
26. 6,000
27. 7,000
28. 5,000
29. 2,000
30. 9,000
31. 2,000
32. 8,000
33. 6,000
34. 7,000
35. 6,000
36. 8,000

Answer Key *(cont.)*

Page 68

Missing parts are as follows:

1. 3, 16, 19, 16, 19, 3, 19, 16
2. 40, 35, 40, 16, 40, 16, 35, 40, 16
3. 7, 8, 6, 8, 7, 8, 6, 8, 6
4. 19, 29, 9, 19, 39, 19, 29, 39
5. circle, rectangle, triangle, circle, circle, rectangle, triangle, rectangle
6. arrow up, arrow left, arrow right, arrow left, arrow right, arrow up, arrow right, arrow up
7. heart, square, circle, square, heart, heart, square
8. horizontal rectangle, vertical rectangle, horizontal rectangle, vertical rectangle, horizontal rectangle, horizontal rectangle, vertical rectangle, vertical rectangle, horizontal rectangle
9. 3, 6, 9, 18, 24, 33
10. 2, 4, 6, 14, 18, 22

Page 69

1. d	2. a	3. d	4. c

Page 70

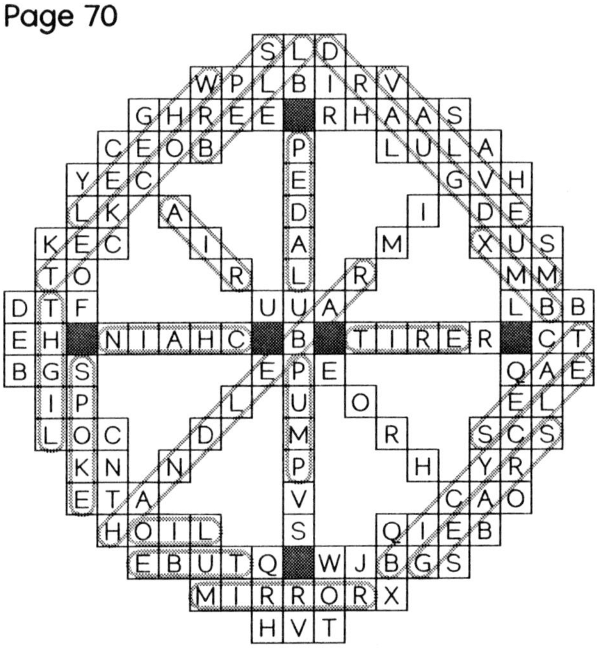

Page 71

1. summer
2. beach
3. splash
4. unicorn
5. lizard

Page 72

1. f, 17	4. e, 8	7. 4	10. 69
2. h, 56	5. d, 13	8. 6	
3. a, 7	6. 10	9. 35	

Page 73

1. It meant that she needed to do her fair share of the work.
2. b
3. c

Page 74

Page 75

3. how many
4. what kind
5. what kind
6. what kind
7. what kind
8. what kind
9. how many
10. what kind
11. how many
12. how many
13. what kind
14. how many
15. how many
16. what kind
17. how many
18. what kind
19. young, old
20. only, pair
21. good, guide
22. many, bird, powerful

Page 76

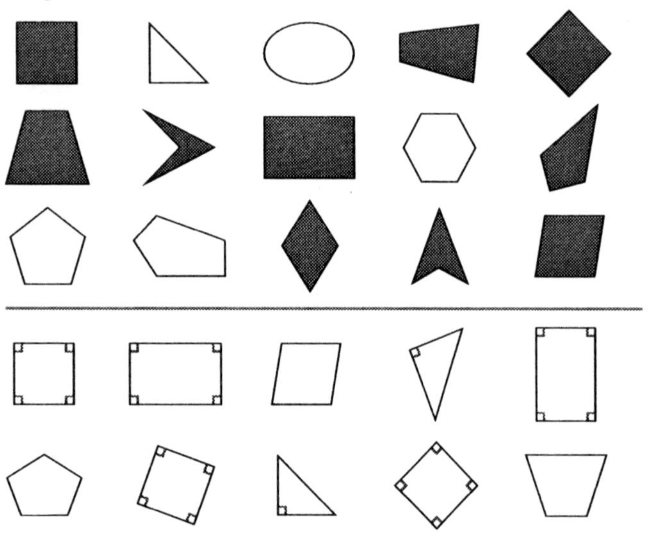

Page 77

1. c
2. In the packet of grass seeds, there must have also been weed seeds.
3. She meowed so the mouse would think she was a cat and get scared.
4. 2 + 1 + 4 + 1 = 8 birds

Page 78

1. $2
2. $6
3. $3\frac{1}{2}$ lbs.
4. $\frac{1}{2}$ lb.
5. $2\frac{1}{2}$ lbs.
6. $3
7. Saturday and Sunday
8. Monday
9. Sunday
10. 460 books

Page 79

Answers will vary. Possible answers:

1. wake
2. dress
3. eat
4. brush teeth
5. leave
6. The dog chased Jenny's cat.
7. The cat raced up the tree.
8. The cat wouldn't come down.
9. Jenny climbed the tree.
10. The cat climbed higher.
11. Jenny climbed higher.
12. Both were too frightened to climb down.

Remaining answers will vary.

Page 80

1. tar/rat
2. raw/war
3. pot/top
4. pets/step
5. live/evil
6. now/won
7. ten/net
8. parts/strap
9. bats/stab
10. drawer/reward

Page 81

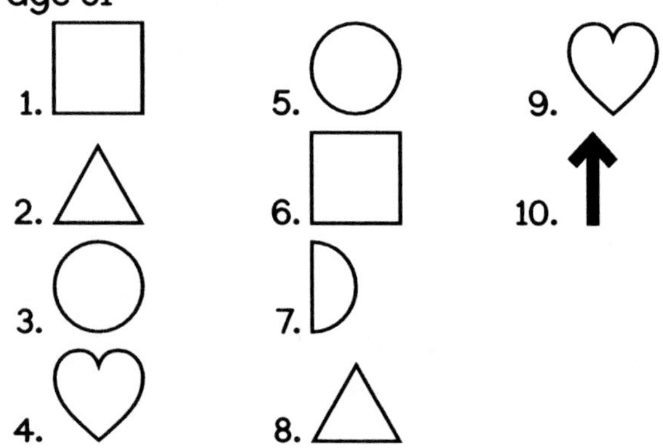

Answer Key *(cont.)*

Page 82

1. blue
2. gold
3. red and yellow
4. purple
5. red, purple, green or yellow, blue, gold
6. classical and jazz
7. heavy metal
8. $\frac{1}{4}$
9. classical and jazz

Page 84

2.

$1 \times \$5.00$
$2 \times \$1.00$
$2 \times \$0.25$
$2 \times \$0.10$
$+\ 3 \times \$0.01$
$\$7.73$

3.

$2 \times \$1.00$
$3 \times \$0.25$
$1 \times \$0.05$
$+\ 2 \times \$0.01$
$\$2.82$

4. $5.68
5. $514.52
6. $162.30
7. $21.45

Page 85

1. b
2. b
3. a
4. c

Page 86

1. 48 hours
2. 7 minutes
3. 6 hours
4. 138 minutes
5. 4 days
6. 165 seconds
7. 3 days
8. 35 days

Page 87

Sentences will vary. Nouns in sentences:

2. frog, mushroom
3. chin, sauce
4. balloon, sky
5. truck, road
6. fruit, basket
7. quarterback, pass, teammate
8. sun, wind, clothes
9. boys, girls, magician
10. office, nurse, child

Page 88

1. 19
2. 37
3. 51
4. 28
5. 50
6. 22
7. 90
8. 29
9. 31
10. 19
11. 12
12. 84
13. 10
14. 7
15. 8
16. 7
17. 5
18. 9
19. 6
20. 2
21. 0
22. 10
23. 12, 21
24. 30, 60
25. 35, 42
26. 30, 35, 40
27. 32, 48, 56

Page 89

1. c
2. the higher risk of getting skin cancer.
3. The UV rays of the sun burn the skin until it turns red and blisters.
4. b

Page 90

2.

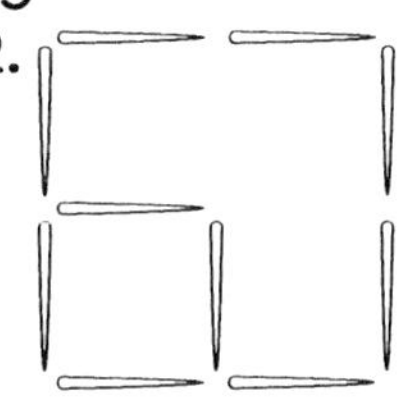

3.

Page 91

I	A	F	I	N	I	S	H	E	D	C
T	L	L	I	E	Y	B	D	O	O	G
S	G	A	E	N	D	E	D	M	O	O
O	L	D	Y	T	A	H	P	I	N	G
V	S	A	M	E	C	L	O	S	E	D
E	U	S	S	R	E	T	A	L	T	O
R	T	H	A	T	I	S	A	L	L	N
G	O	N	E	C	O	M	E	T	O	E
A	N	D	E	I	M	O	U	T	N	D

What Do You See?: All good things must come to an end.

Reward Chart